Beyond Turtle Graphics

Further Explorations of Logo

David D. Thornburg

Addison-Wesley Publishing Company
Menlo Park, California • Reading, Massachusetts
Wokingham, Berkshire, U.K. • Amsterdam • Don Mills, Ontario • Sydney

Acknowledgments

Page 136 from *Computer Power and Human Reasoning: From Judgment to Calculation* by J. Weizenbaum, pp. 3, 4. (1976) W. H. Freeman and Company. Copyright © 1976.

An ancient Sufi Tale and "Duck Soup" from *The Exploits of the Incomparable Mulla Nasrudin* by Idries Shah, pp. 104, 107. © 1983 Designist Communications. The Octagon Press Ltd., U.K.

Cover Design: Victoria Ann Philp

This book is published by the Addison-Wesley Innovative Division

*To my father for his encouragement
of my inquisitiveness and for teaching me
the peace of fishing*

Other books by David Thornburg:

Picture This!

Picture This Too!

The KoalaPad Book

Discovering Apple Logo

Exploring Logo Without a Computer

Computer Art and Animation:
A User's Guide to Atari Logo

Computer Art and Animation:
A User's Guide to Commodore 64 Logo

Computer Art and Animation:
A User's Guide to TI-99/4A Color Logo

Computer Art and Animation:
A User's Guide to Radio Shack Color Logo

Preface

Like many other personal computer enthusiasts, you have probably heard about the language called Logo. You may think that Logo is a "kid's" language, or that it is useful only for the creation of pictures. If this is your impression of Logo, this book will surprise you. Yes, it is true that some aspects of Logo can be mastered by youngsters in the second grade, just as it is true that Logo can be used to make stunning pictures on the display screen. But these two aspects of Logo have over-shadowed a far more important point: that Logo is a complete programming language suitable for a wide range of programming tasks. In fact, it is the only widely available computer language on personal computers that lets programmers assemble complex systems ranging from the generation of new computer languages to the exploration of topics in the field of artificial intelligence.

Even if Logo didn't have all this power, consider the fact that your Logo procedures will remain legible to you six months after you have written them. This feature alone should be quite attractive to most BASIC programmers.

There is another reason you should be learning about the non-graphic aspects of Logo at this time. We are entering an era when many applications of computers are devoted to the manipulation of non-numerical information. In addition to working with numbers, computers are dealing with text, logical ideas, hunches, etc. Although much of the research into new ways of using computers is being sponsored by government projects (such as the Japanese fifth generation effort) or in university or industrial laboratories, each of us who uses a personal computer can take part in explorations in this arena on our own. But to do this we must choose the correct programming language. In fact, the choice of a programming language can be far more important than the choice of the computer used to execute the programs.

Ever since the introduction of the personal computer to the general public, we have been encouraged to learn BASIC. Using BASIC for more than numerical programming tasks is like typing with your tongue—it can be done, but the effort is overwhelming. The fact of the matter is that our choice of a computer language can influence the very types of problems we are willing to solve. One of the beautiful things about Logo is that in addition to providing a rich assortment of objects with which we can compute, it allows us to define both our own operations for these objects and new types of computational objects and even to construct entirely new computer languages of our own design.

If this seems slightly overwhelming to you, bear with me. Although Logo lets you do many fancy things, it is no harder to learn than any other high-level language such as BASIC. A side effect of learning to program in Logo is that it eases the way for you to learn other useful languages like Pascal, C, LISP, and PROLOG.

"But," you say, "is this the same Logo that kids use to draw circles and houses with turtle graphics?"

Yes, it is. But the problem with most people's introduction to Logo is that once they learn how to draw pictures they stop before finding that they have left 90 percent of the language unexplored. And, so, we come to the reason I wrote this book.

I use computers a lot, and I like to create my own programs. Because some of the programs I create are virtually impossible for me to write in BASIC, I gravitated to Logo before it was trendy to do so. I had to teach myself the non-graphics portion of this language and was frustrated to see many fine books on intermediate and advanced BASIC programming but to find almost nothing about intermediate Logo programming. This book is designed to help fill this gap. I have written the book I wish I could have read a few years ago.

In my writing I have made some assumptions about you. For example, I assume that:

- You have a computer or have access to one.
- You have heard about Logo and may know about turtle-graphics programming.

- You have written some programs of your own in the past, probably in BASIC.
- You are ready to explore some new ideas.

If you are completely new to computer programming, you might want to start with a book on turtle graphics programming, such as *Discovering Apple Logo* by the author (Addison-Wesley, 1983), to get the flavor of this language. Once you know a little bit about Logo you will be ready for this book.

To be of practical use, this book needs to focus on a version of Logo that you can use. Although many of the procedures and projects in this book work with other versions of the language, I have chosen Apple Logo II as the implementation language. This version of Logo can be used with either the Apple IIc or an Apple IIe computer with the extended 80-column card (to provide 128 K bytes of RAM). I have used this version of Logo for this book for two reasons. First, Apple Logo II has several features that make it an excellent Logo for list-processing applications; second, this version of the language leaves plenty of workspace for your own procedures. Of course, you will find yourself wanting even more workspace, but that is a desire common to all who program computers.

Since I have mentioned the *why* and *how* aspects of this book, it is time to tell you *what* it covers. I start by describing the history and mythology of Logo and compare Logo to BASIC, because BASIC is such a commonly used programming environment. Next, I discuss Logo's programming style. The style of a program can not only make the listing easier to understand but it can also influence your thinking about problem solving. I also try to provide a context—a reason for introducing topics in the first place. It is not the goal of this book to replace the reference manual. Instead the goal is to illustrate the power of Logo by describing applications that you may actually use.

Although this is not a turtle graphics book, I use the turtle-graphics environment to explore some of the more challenging programming concepts in Logo (especially recursion) and to illustrate the creation of new computational objects. Beyond that, we will explore computing with numbers, words, lists, and objects of our own design and will conclude with the creation of a new programming language, written in Logo. We will even explore the kinds of programs we can write in this new language.

Once you have finished this book you will be ready to tackle an unlimited range of projects on your own in fields ranging from entertainment applications to database systems to artificial intelligence. You will also have developed a programming style that will serve you well as you learn other computer languages.

I am happy to say that I am not alone in my enthusiasm for Logo as a language for serious non-graphics applications. In fact, friends of mine—like James Milojkovic and Jim McCauley—have been very vocal in their encouragement in this area. I am indebted to them for their support. John Allen has helped this project without knowing it by writing a book on artificial intelligence that has stimulated more lunch conversations than I can count.

One of the most vocal Logo supporters I know is Ian Browde, a man of many talents who has the courage to view learning and Logo with the sense of wonder and enthusiasm usually found only in children. Our conversations over the past two years have ranged over such topics as robotics, the Apple Color Plotter, Sufi stories, his experiences teaching on a kibbutz, the proper way to assemble a salad, and our shared dreams for a world in which the quest for knowledge is the nutrient of us all. Thank you, Ian; I hope you have enjoyed our conversations as much as I have!

Pat Calderhead at Apple Computer has supported this project from its inception and has been of tremendous help under circumstances that were, at times, most bizarre. Her assistance, along with Ian's and others at Apple, has made this book a reality, and I am indebted to them and their colleagues for their help.

But, most of all, I am indebted to my wife, Pam, for her support and the creation of an environment of love and understanding in which creativity blossoms effortlessly.

To all of you, I convey my deepest thanks.

Monterey, California   *D.T.*
March 1985

Contents

I. Logo—More than Pretty Pictures

Why Learn Programming in the First Place?

This book is devoted to the exploration of computer programming. Because of the broad and yet eclectic nature of this topic, we might do well to start by exploring the reasons anyone would want to learn how to program a computer in the first place.

People give many reasons for learning to program. For many of us, it is an intellectual skill—a hobby, perhaps. The very act of conveying instructions to a machine and then seeing those instructions carried out can be entertaining and enlightening all at the same time. Of course there are many other reasons for learning to program. For some it is a professional activity. We create programs to be used by other people who have neither the time nor the inclination to learn the craft of programming themselves. We also write programs to satisfy our own software needs that aren't met by commercially available packages.

But, as anyone who has programmed knows, there is a special sensation that comes from creating a set of instructions that are then executed by the computer. It is a feeling that cannot be explained to one who hasn't tried it. Some measure of this feeling was expressed by Frederick Brooks in his book *The Mythical Man-Month*:

The programmer, like the poet, works only slightly removed from pure thought-stuff. He builds castles in the air, from air, creating by exertion of the imagination. Few media of creation are so flexible, so easy to polish and rework, so readily capable of realizing grand conceptual structures. . . .

Yet the program construct, unlike the poet's words, is real in the sense that it moves and works, producing visible outputs separate from the construct itself. It prints results, draws pictures, produces sounds, moves arms. The magic of myth and legend has come true in our time. One types the correct incantation on a keyboard, and a display screen comes to life, showing things that never were nor could be.

This creation of what never was is one of the greatest joys of programming. The computer programmer is able to construct new worlds in the computer, model ideas, conduct experiments, and ask and then answer "What if?" The flexibility of this medium is fantastic. One can create graphic images one minute, music the next, and perform complex calculations after that—all on the same computer, and all through the use of the same programming environment.

Most of you already know these things, but it is especially important that we all start at a point from which we can see that programming not only lets us perform experiments on the computer but also lets us see how the development of programming style and skill can help us to become better critical thinkers, whether or not we use computers.

Programming has value in that it lets us use the computer as a lever for the mind—a tool to help us think better, just as a crowbar helps our hands open crates or a bicycle helps our legs move us farther faster. Far from replacing the human intellect, the computer can make us better thinkers. If it had no other consequence than this, computer programming would be a worthwhile activity.

Programming takes place in a context: our programs need goals. It also takes place in a programming environment, what we call the computer language. The context and language are not separable from one another, although claims have been made that some computer languages are general purpose in nature. Many businesses use programs written in COBOL; many scientists use FORTRAN, many professional software developers use languages like C, Pascal, and FORTH; and researchers in the field of artificial intelligence use languages like LISP and PROLOG. This book is about none of these languages, and yet parts of it are about all of them.

This is a book about a language called Logo—not the level

of Logo that stops at simple turtle-graphic images, but the level that takes us beyond turtle graphics to the realm where we can construct our own computational objects and write our own computer languages. We will explore Logo as a language in which one can create programs for music, poetry, and arithmetic as well as graphic images.

For Logo, the context is diffuse. One can create "practical" programs in it, or one can use Logo to create entertainment, business, and professional software. Beyond that, one can use Logo to explore topics in the domain of artificial intelligence. A characteristic of Logo that gives it such broad applicability is the freedom it gives the programmer to determine just how knowledge is to be represented in the computer. This capability, along with the freedom to create new extensions of Logo with Logo itself, makes it a good language to learn in its own right as well as a stepping stone to other high-level languages such as Pascal, C, LISP, and PROLOG.

To better understand this wider view of Logo, we explore its background and capabilities in the remainder of this chapter.

Logo's Background and Potential

Logo has two roots, one philosophical and the other computational. In order to understand the power and utility of Logo, it helps to know a bit about these roots.

The name that is inextricably linked with Logo is that of Seymour Papert. Based on his own experiences as a child, Papert came to believe that what and how children learn are directly influenced by the materials and models available to them. He further developed these ideas in his study with Jean Piaget at the Center for Genetic Epistemology in Geneva in the early 1960s. Piaget's theories of learning influenced Papert strongly and reinforced his belief that a child learns spontaneously by encountering and manipulating the environment. To Papert, the materials provided to the child are of major importance in determining the direction of the child's education. The computer had the potential, in his mind, of being a particularly valuable tool with which a child could make discoveries. But in order to be useful, this tool had to be accessible to the learner, which meant that the computer needed to be provided with a computer language that fostered experimentation, that didn't interfere with the problem-solving process. The language needed to be sufficiently rich to allow users to experiment with different types of information and operations and to develop new representations of information and new types of operations on their own. The environment that Papert envisioned for young children was one that would be warmly embraced by sophisticated computer users of all ages. For example, it was important that the language not be restricted to working with numbers but that it should be capable of working with other types of information as well. The language had to work with symbolic expressions of all types.

At the time Logo was being designed, the principal language that worked with symbolic expressions was LISP. LISP is a symbol-manipulation language that has been used by a large part of the university and industrial research community to explore topics in the field of artificial intelligence. Unlike Logo, LISP was not designed to be accessible to children. It was, however, designed to let programmers create new computational objects on their own, develop their own structure for representing knowledge, and create their own extensions of the language. In fact, LISP contained much of what Logo needed. As a result, Logo resembles LISP in many ways but is also different from LISP in several areas. The differences between Logo and LISP are not important for what we will explore in this book. What *is* important is that Logo contains much of what makes languages like LISP so powerful to those who are engaged in advanced studies in computer science.

By taking its philosophical underpinnings from models on how children learn and its computational underpinnings from LISP, Logo is in fact a language suitable for all ages and for the exploration of many computational areas. One can start using Logo within a few minutes of sitting at the computer keyboard, but there is no upper limit to the types of problems to which Logo can be applied. This makes Logo unique as a programming language.

Logo and BASIC—A Comparison

Thus far I have said nothing about the computer language BASIC. Given that BASIC is probably the most generally available language on the market today, it is important that Logo and BASIC be compared side by side. Many common misconceptions are often expressed about Logo, and many people feel that someone who starts with Logo's turtle graphics should then "graduate" to learning BASIC for "serious" applications. In order to set some of these misconceptions to rest, I will address several aspects of Logo and BASIC in a very general way. I therefore hope to show some of the differences between these two languages and hope to change the attitude that Logo is only for children or for creating images.

How Easy Are These Languages to Learn?

Both Logo and BASIC let the user start writing programs within a short time of encountering the language. The normal starting point for a Logo user is to learn about turtle graphics and use this tool for creating complex geometric patterns on the display. Most introductions to BASIC start by having the user write programs that accept textual information from the keyboard and display information on the screen. From this point one typically introduces the arithmetic aspects of BASIC into programs. Once one advances past these starting points, both languages require some effort to master. The difference is that much of the advanced BASIC programming involves getting "close" to the computer (changing the contents of certain memory locations, for example). Because BASIC is not a procedure-oriented language, complex BASIC programs tend to be quite large. This, coupled with the use of line numbers as labels, makes BASIC programs hard to read. In order to master the non-graphics portion of Logo a user learns a few general principles and then constructs new Logo commands and operations from these principles and from Logo's set of primitive commands.

Do These Languages Let Us Add New Commands to Their Vocabularies?

This is one area in which BASIC and Logo are very different from each other. Languages like BASIC are enclosed in locked boxes that cannot be opened by the user. Logo, on the other hand, is like a lump of clay in that it can be molded and formed into any environment we want to create. BASIC provides a fixed set of primitive commands and operations out of which we must make our program. Logo lets us define new commands and operations that are treated just as if they were part of the original language. This feature has important stylistic consequences when one is writing Logo programs. The act of programming in Logo is in reality the act of defining new Logo commands and operations. Once these procedures have been created, the user can invoke any of them by simply typing their names. In BASIC only one program or procedure is in the workspace at a time. In Logo many procedures are typically in the workspace, any of which can be run by typing its name and any of which can be used by any other procedure in the workspace. This capability of Logo to accept new words into its vocabulary is called *extensibility*. It is a feature shared by natural languages such as English. English serves us well because we can add new words to its vocabulary. For example, if the English vocabulary had no new words added since the 1600s, we would find it cumbersome, if not impossible, to use in daily conversation.

One of the reasons extensibility is important is that the nature of our language can influence our very thoughts. Logo has the freedom to grow with our thoughts.

How Do These Languages Treat Variables?

Variables in BASIC are global, so they are available to all parts of the program at the same time. This may seem to be the appropriate way to do things, and for some of the information we store in variables it is. But many times we want to use variables to store information temporarily in one part of a program while it is calculating a result to be used by another part of the program. If all variables are global, you must be very careful to choose names that are not used anywhere else in the system. For small programs this isn't hard, but for large programs containing lots of subroutines, this can be quite a chore. Logo, on the other hand, lets us use both global and local variables. Local variables preserve their values inside the procedure in which they are used. Once this procedure is exited, the variable ceases to exist. In addition to making the naming of variables easier, local variables are a key component to a very powerful Logo tool called recursive programming.

Another major difference in the way BASIC and Logo treat variables is that when a global variable is created in Logo, the system assumes we want to preserve its value for later use. Consequently, when we save our Logo workspace we not only save the procedures we have created but we also save the names and values of the global variables. Most versions of BASIC, on the other hand, save only the BASIC program itself. If we want to save data as well, we must either create a separate data file or incorporate our global data into our program through the use of DATA statements.

How Do These Languages Treat Recursive Programs?

When an element of the procedure definition contains references to the procedure itself, it is called a recursive procedure. Recursion is a major programming tool in Logo, and the ability to think in terms of recursive procedures can simplify the solution of problems that would be quite cumbersome to solve otherwise. Many of the procedures we create in this book are recursive. Because of Logo's roots in LISP, recursion is a natural part of the language. BASIC does not support recursion in the general sense of the word and is thus missing a tool that can make complex programming tasks quite easy to implement.

What Types of Data Are Used by These Languages?

BASIC uses two general types of data: numbers and character strings. In some versions of BASIC numbers appear in several forms: integer, single-precision decimal, and double-precision decimal. Logo works with three types of data: numbers, words, and lists. There is little difference between the ways the two languages treat numbers. A Logo word is similar in some respects to a BASIC string. The Logo list is an assembly of numbers, words, or other lists. One might be tempted to compare the list to an array in BASIC, but this comparison would not be accurate. Because Logo procedures and primitives are themselves represented by Logo words, lists can contain information ranging from data to executable programs. This capability makes it easy to write Logo procedures that generate and execute *other* Logo procedures. The construction of self-modifying programs is virtually impossible in BASIC.

How Do These Languages Handle Arithmetic?

Both BASIC and Logo come equipped to perform a wide range of mathematical computations, and both languages are typically endowed with at least the commonly used transcendental functions (sine, cosine, etc.). Whereas some versions of BASIC let us define functions of our own, this capability is innate in Logo.

What Restrictions Do These Languages Impose on Variable Names?

Logo uses words as variable names. As a result, a variable can be given any name we want to use—FISH, NEXT ANSWER, A25X, GEORGES BROTHERS RESPONSE, etc. Most versions of BASIC do not give us this freedom. For example, a variable name in Applesoft BASIC may be up to 238 characters long, but this version of the language ignores any characters after the first two. This means that we could have two variables named APPLE and APRICOT in our listing, and they would be considered the same when we ran the program. A further restriction is that a BASIC variable name cannot have any of BASIC's key words imbedded in it. For example, we cannot have variables named WAITER, FRENCH, GROWTH, RESPONSE, BEND, or FOREIGN because WAIT, FRE, GR, ON, END, and FOR are all BASIC keywords.

Because carefully chosen variable names can make our programs legible to others, there are merits in being able to choose our own variable names without restrictions.

How Legible Are the Program Listings in These Languages?

As normally printed, long Logo listings and long BASIC listings can be equally obscure. One legibility advantage that Logo might have comes from the fact that most Logo programmers create a program out of an assembly of several small procedures. Because these smaller procedures are self-contained and are typically only a few lines long, each of them is fairly easy to read.

Do These Languages Encourage the Development of a Particular Programming Style?

Programming style can and should be taught. One can write elegant programs in BASIC and rambling messes in Logo. For programmers who are concerned about stylistic issues, Logo has some advantages over BASIC in that it encourages procedural thinking. In top-down programming, for example, the problem solution is expressed by a procedure that calls a set of subprocedures that solve each part of the problem. Each of these subprocedures may use other subprocedures. This style of programming can be simulated in BASIC through the careful use of subroutines, but it is easier to grasp when it is implemented in Logo.

How Do Logo and BASIC Facilitate the Learning of Other Computer Languages?

Because of the freedom Logo gives the programmer in defining new procedures, creating variable names, and generally structuring the representation of knowledge in the computer, Logo programmers may have an easier time than BASIC programmers in learning languages like LISP, PROLOG, and FORTH. The discipline of procedural programming is also a valuable asset when learning languages like Pascal and C. However, if one has learned a structured approach to writing BASIC programs, the transition from BASIC to other languages shouldn't be much harder.

Why Does Logo Cost So Much—After All, Isn't BASIC Free?

It is true that BASIC comes with the Apple computer, but this doesn't make it free. BASIC is a language we end up paying for, whether we want it or not. The price of BASIC for computers that don't include it with the system, is comparable to the price of Logo.

The real cost of a computer language must be measured in the amount of time one has to spend accomplishing a programming task. It is likely that Logo is far cheaper than BASIC when measured in this manner.

How This Book Works

This book concentrates on the exploration of Logo's capabilities for intermediate-level programmers. The approach is based on the idea that Logo lets us compute with various types of objects. Some of the chapters cover the properties and applications of certain Logo objects, and other chapters cover applications that go beyond structures native to Logo. Because this book deals with stylistic issues as well as practical examples, I occasionally go off on a tangent. When I feel a digression coming on I will direct you to appendix 2, where all my digressions have been stored. This way, you can avoid my rambling comments if you want and stick to the bread-and-butter items. I have endeavored to put the digressions into self-contained sections so that they can be read at any time.

Because comput*ing* is such an exciting topic by itself, it is a shame that we have to cloud the issue by worrying about the comput*er*. Because this book is useful with Apple Logo II running on either the Apple IIc or IIe computers, because these computers are a little different from each other, and because there are a lot of peculiar mechanical details to be mastered, appendix 1 is devoted to the mechanisms of using Logo. This includes setting up the system, creating file disks, and using the printer. By placing these details in the appendix, I assume that you are already familiar with Logo II, PRODOS, and the Imagewriter printer as you read the rest of the book. This lets us keep the body of the book focused on the key issue: exploring the Logo beyond turtle graphics!

II. An Introduction to Logo's Style

The Importance of Style

Programming languages are flexible enough to allow individual programming styles. A programming style isn't forced (or at least it shouldn't be); it is like a writing style in that it should evolve as one's skill with the language grows. It should adapt to new problems and new activities. Some languages encourage the development of certain styles, but in general each of us is free to choose from a variety of ways of structuring our ideas when we write programs.

The importance of style becomes clearer when we understand the function of programming. Presumably, one starts with a problem to be solved with the computer. The goal is to transform the problem into a program that embodies the solution. This transformation requires developing a model for the solution of the problem and creating a transformation of this model into the computer program itself. Rather than treating the problem and program as two distinct entities, it is useful to think of the program as a metamorphosis of the problem.

This metamorphosis is aided by some conceptual models of how the computer performs its tasks. These models don't have to deal with the bits and bytes of the computer; in fact, they don't even have to be accurate—but they must be consistent with observations of the computer's behavior when it is given instructions. It is the dialog between the user and the computer that is important. A well-designed computer language can support the kinds of dialogs that help the user develop procedures for solving problems.

As we explore Logo I will be proposing some models of how this language works. These models are chosen to make it easy for us to solve problems with Logo, not because they are representative of how Logo actually works. They reflect a particular programming style, one that may prove useful to you.

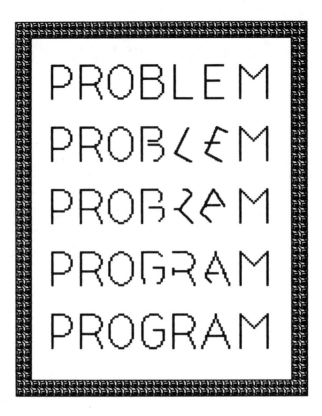

But keep in mind that a style exists to help you, not to hold you back. I have seen many examples of programs written by purists who force their programs into a particular style, even if it makes the operation of the program hard to understand. This may appear elegant to some people, but it seems silly to me.

And so the style of a program is like the style of architecture—it is a matter of taste. But just as architectural styles are influenced by the construction materials available, programming styles are influenced by the components and syntax of the language we are using. We should then start by exploring the way Logo works.

The Structure of Logo Commands

Logo is a computer language made from building blocks called *procedures*. Quite a few procedures are already built into the language; these are called *primitives*. One of Logo's strong points is that it lets us build our own procedures that are treated by Logo just the same as if they were primitives. This feature of Logo is called *extensibility*.

Logo procedures are of two types: *commands* and *operations*. A command is an instruction for Logo to do something that is self-contained (to print something on the screen or to play a game, for example). An operation, on the other hand, is an instruction for Logo to perform some activity that produces a result that is passed to another procedure. For example, one might use an operation to calculate the cube root of a number. The result of this operation could be combined with other operations to produce the result of a complex calculation that would then be printed on the screen. Although they are in no way restricted to mathematical activities, operations resemble mathematical functions. As we will see later, the Logo primitive that is a universal component of operations is OUTPUT. (*Note:* In the remainder of this book, Logo primitives and other characters that are likely to appear on the display screen are shown in this type face.)

There is a special kind of Logo operation called a *predicate*. The outputs from a predicate are one of two words: TRUE or FALSE. These words can be used by certain Logo commands (called *conditional commands*) to alter the flow of a Logo program. Predicates test some state or condition in the system and pass the results of this test to another procedure. Logo comes equipped with some predicates of its own, and we are free to create others. Most Logo predicates end in the letter P, as in EQUALP, EMPTYP, etc. This convention is a carryover from LISP. In fact, a true LISP hacker is likely to see if a friend wants lunch by coming into her office and asking

HUNGRYP?

We will make extensive use of predicates in our Logo programs.

In addition to having two kinds of procedures, Logo comes equipped with several types of *data objects*, which have a wide variety of uses. They can represent simple types of data, such as numbers or sentences, and they can be used to represent other forms of information ranging from musical scores to logical syllogisms. In fact, part of the task in writing Logo programs is deciding how knowledge is to be represented inside our program. Logo's data objects let us represent anything we can model.

The three types of data with which Logo works are *numbers*, *words*, and *lists*. If we were purists (and we shouldn't be), we wouldn't distinguish much between numbers and words.

Logo numbers resemble the numbers we encounter every day: integers and decimals. Integer numbers are typically used for enumerating things, such as counting parts in a bin and representing the number of people on a team. Decimal numbers, on the other hand, are used for measuring things that have a value chosen along a continuum, such as the weight of a sack of potatoes. Unlike some computer languages, Logo doesn't make a big deal out of the type of number you are using, although some of Logo's mathematical operations always produce integers and others always produce decimals. We encounter examples of these as we progress.

A Logo word is just a collection of alphanumeric characters with no embedded spaces. The names of all Logo procedures are words, as are the names of any variables you might create. Because Logo words can be the names of procedures and variables or can stand alone as words themselves, they are very useful data objects.

Probably the most powerful data object in Logo is the list. A list is a collection of numbers, words, or other lists that is enclosed in square brackets. For example:

[cow horse sheep dog harpsichord]

is a list of words, and

[3.1415 Henry [take out the garbage when you get home]]

is a list containing a number, a word, and another list. A list can be used for grouping a set of Logo procedures that are to be executed a certain number of times. For example,

REPEAT 4 [FORWARD 50 RIGHT 90]

A list can also be used to build new data objects of the user's own design.

Now that we know Logo uses procedures and data objects, we need to know how these are combined to produce a Logo expression. Logo expressions generally are of the *prefix* form, which means that the command or operation precedes the data objects to be used by the procedure. For example, if we wanted to print the sum of 4 and 5 we would enter:

PRINT SUM 4 5

This line is interpreted by Logo in the following way. PRINT knows that it is to print what follows it on the screen. The word after print is a Logo operation called SUM. In order for SUM to give information to PRINT, it needs two numbers to add together. These two numbers appear after the word SUM, so it adds them together and passes the result (9) to PRINT, which then meets its responsibility to the system by printing the result on the screen for us to see.

All Logo expressions can be read from left to right. Keep in mind that certain parts of the expression may have to wait for later parts to perform their chore first (as in our example).

Prefix commands are not the only type used by computer languages. FORTH, for example, uses *postfix* commands. Our example above would be written in FORTH as:

This form is sometimes called RPN, or Reverse Polish Notation. There are rumors of another variant called ORTHFAY that includes RPN and PLS (Pig Latin Syntax), but I haven't seen this form in use.

In addition to its prefix forms, Logo has some operations that appear in the *infix* form. This is the familiar form we usually use when doing arithmetic.

PRINT 3 + 9

Infix operations appear as a convenience for us as programmers, so we should use them. Logo purists can avoid them if they want.

There is one other detail of Logo we should address at this point: Logo variables. The concept of a variable is hard for some people to grasp. If the following brief treatment doesn't seem clear, I have a more detailed digression on this topic in appendix 2.

A variable can be thought of as a box. The box has two parts, a name and a contents. The variable name is a Logo word, and the contents can be any data object we desire—a number, a word, or a list. One way to create a variable is with the Logo **MAKE** command. For example:

MAKE "John [president of the corporation]

The quotation mark before the word **John** indicates that we are making the literal word **John** the name of the variable. This is somewhat similar to our use of quotation marks in English:

''Horse'' is a word made with five letters.

as opposed to

I think my horse should have won the race.

The **MAKE** command has the task of *binding* our contents (in this case, the list [president of the corporation]) to a word (in our case, John). So, to use our box analogy, John is the *name* of the box, and [president of the corporation] is the *contents* of the box. We can examine the thing that is in the variable through the use of the Logo operation called **THING**. For example:

PRINT THING ''John

will produce

president of the corporation

If we omitted **THING**, we would be asking Logo to print the word John. In other words:

PRINT ''John

will produce

John

Because we often want to refer to the thing contained in a variable, Logo provides us with a shorthand way of doing this.

PRINT :John

is equivalent to

PRINT THING ''John

By replacing the quotation mark with a colon (:), we inform Logo that we are referring to the item bound to the word **John** rather than to the word **John** itself.

Variables that are created with the **MAKE** command are called *global variables*. Their values are accessible to all Logo procedures in the system, and their values will be stored on the disk along with our Logo procedures when we save our workspace. Logo programs also make extensive use of *local variables*— storage boxes that exist only within the confines of a single procedure. Once the procedure ends, these variables disappear. The values stored in local variables can be transferred from one procedure to another (I will show how later), but the variable name itself will vanish.

If this all seems a bit esoteric, please bear with me. The goal here is to present an overview of the major Logo tools. The rest of this book shows how they might be used, and the examples should clarify any concerns you may have at this point.

But before exploring Logo procedures in depth, I would like to describe a strategy I use when solving a problem with Logo. This strategy is not universally applicable, but it works well most of the time.

A Strategy for Program Design

When I set out to create a solution to a problem, I start by exploring the types of objects the problem deals with. For example, in designing the music system described in a later chapter, I decided that the basic data object should be a *musical score*. I then had to choose a *representation* for this object. (It ended up being a list, but this isn't always going to be the case.) Once the structure of this object was designed, I then specified the types of operations that were to be performed on this object (for example, I wanted to **PLAY** the score, to **TRANSPOSE** it, etc.). After I had defined the representation of the score, it was fairly easy to develop a consistent set of procedures, any of which could deal with this representation.

Sometimes I find that my first choice for representing an

object has some serious flaws, and I have to redefine the representation before proceeding with the definition of the operations themselves. Nonetheless, I find that defining the structure of the data is best done before creating any of the rest of the program.

The next chapter explores some of Logo's powerful tools with a computational object you may already know—Logo's turtle.

III.   Computing with Turtles

After commenting so extensively on the power of Logo beyond turtle graphics, it may seem a bit confusing to see this chapter included in this book. The main reason it is included is that Logo's turtle is a perfect tool for exploring several programming ideas that we will use in most of our activities. Because Logo activities using the turtle can be traced visually, it is sometimes easier to use the turtle to explain these concepts than it is to explain them in other ways.

There are three topics on which we will focus our attention in this chapter: computational objects, user-defined procedures, and recursion.

The Turtle as a Computational Object

Logo allows us to create graphic images on the screen through the use of an imaginary character called the turtle. If we give Logo a command to clear the graphic screen by entering

CLEARSCREEN

or

CS

a representation of the turtle will appear on the display.

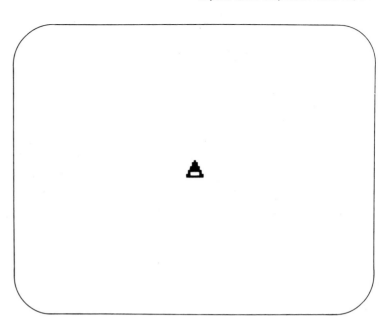

The turtle (displayed as a solid triangle) is an example of a *computational object*. It creates pictures on the display screen by responding to *messages* that have been sent to it by the user. The turtle can receive several types of messages.

One type of message alters the turtle's state. For example, the turtle can be moved forward and backward with the commands FORWARD (or FD) and BACK (or BK), and it can be turned to the left or right with the commands LEFT (or LT) and RIGHT (or RT). In addition to these incremental commands, there are messages or commands that cause the turtle to assume a newly prescribed state, independent of its previous state. These commands affect the turtle's screen position (HOME, SETPOS, SETX, and SETY), its heading (SETHEADING) and its visibility (HIDETURTLE and SHOWTURTLE).

Another type of turtle message pertains to activities involving lines on the display screen. Among the more common of these are instructions to lift and lower the turtle's pen (PENUP or PU, and PENDOWN or PD). The color of the turtle's pen can be chosen with the SETPC command. Other commands can erase the contents of the screen (CLEAN), fill an area that encloses the turtle (FILL), and place a dot at a specified screen position (DOT).

Other messages let you gather information about the turtle's state, the state of the turtle's pen, or the state of the screen. These include operations to give the turtle's position and heading (XCOR, YCOR, POS, and HEADING), whether or not the turtle is visible (SHOWNP), the state of the turtle's pen (PEN) and color (PENCOLOR), and whether or not the turtle is sitting over a dot on the screen (DOTP).

There are turtle messages other than those mentioned above, but this list shows how versatile the turtle object is. The combination of the turtle *object* and the set of turtle *messages* allows you to create a wide variety of images on the display screen.

Drawing pictures on Logo's display screen can be thought of as sending appropriate messages to the turtle. As the turtle receives and obeys these messages, a picture will be drawn. For example, the command:

REPEAT 5 [FD 80 RT 144]

instructs the turtle to trace a path that outlines a five-point star. If the pen is down when the turtle moves, an image of the star will be drawn on the screen. (If the image appears somewhat squashed on your display screen, refer to the SETSCRUNCH command in appendix 1.)

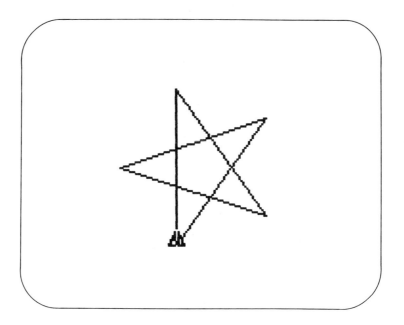

At any time we can make inquiries about the state of the turtle. As discussed in a later chapter, we can use copies of this status information to create our own representations of the turtle. By making several representations of turtles within Logo, we are able to simulate the existence of an entire herd of turtles, each of which is able to wander in its own path.

The concept of the turtle as a computational object is an important one. Sometimes it is easy to fall into the trap of thinking that computations can be performed only on numbers. In the broader realm of symbol manipulation, a computational object can be anything on which we want to perform operations. We operate on the turtle by sending it messages that change its state. We operate on numbers by adding them together and performing other traditional manipulations on them. We can operate on words and lists by taking them apart and building them up, and we can operate on arbitrary shapes by rotating them, reflecting them in mirrors, and translating them. In fact, anything can be a computational object if we can define a representation for the object in Logo and create a set of operations that change its state or produce a result of interest to us.

As mentioned in the previous chapter, the ability to create our own objects and operations will be very useful as we use Logo to solve certain problems.

The Power of Procedures

Logo interprets anything typed at the keyboard as an instruction to be carried out immediately. If we were to enter the command:

```
REPEAT 4 [FD 89 RT 90]
```

a square would be drawn as soon as we pressed the return key. Quite often we will want to create a series of expressions whose execution is to be deferred until a later time. Logo accommodates us by letting us cluster a set of Logo expressions under one name. The task of binding a collection of Logo expressions to a name is called defining a procedure.

There are two major ways to define procedures in Logo. The pure way is with the DEFINE command, and the normal way is with the TO command. Because DEFINE is generally used only when a Logo procedure is being written by another procedure, or when the procedure is written by a LISP enthusiast, we will concentrate on the use of the TO command.

To start in an innocuous fashion, suppose we wanted to create lots of stars of different sizes and we were tired of entering commands like the following each time we wanted a star to appear on the screen:

```
REPEAT 5 [FD 83 RT 144]
```

We could make life easier by entering a procedure such as:

```
TO STAR :size
REPEAT 5 [FD :size RT 144]
END
```

This procedure uses a local variable called size. Because we never refer to size by its name but only as a value to be used within the procedure, we don't use the quotation mark when referring to size. For example, we might use this procedure by typing

STAR 50

to draw a star with sides 50 units long; the value (50) is passed inside the procedure through the local variable size and is used in the FD command to determine how far the turtle should go forward. Once the procedure is finished, this instance of the variable size disappears.

Now that we have created a procedure (STAR), we should examine the consequences of our action. We have:

- Created a new word in Logo's vocabulary.
- Created a building block that can be used by other Logo procedures.
- Written a Logo program.
- Reduced the effort needed to draw a star on the screen.

Because Logo programs are built out of assemblages of procedures, one way to view the task of Logo programming is as the defining of the procedures that, when invoked, will operate a program. For example, we might define a game program that would be started by typing

START

The START procedure might be defined as follows:

```
TO START
SET.UP.PLAYING.FIELD
GIVE.INSTRUCTIONS
ASK.FOR.PLAYER.INFORMATION
SETUP.GAMES.PARAMETERS
PLAY.GAME
UPDATE.HIGH.SCORE
DISPLAY.ENDING.MESSAGES
END
```

This procedure is simply a set of other procedures that carry out part of the tasks to be performed by the game program. Each of these tasks can be a self-contained procedure that can be written and tested independently of the others. Each of these procedures may use even more user-defined procedures, until the final set of procedures are built from Logo primitives and procedures already defined. This approach is called *top-down* programming. The game is expressed as a set of procedures, each of which is made from subprocedures, and so on. The goal in top-down programming is to break the task into "mind-sized" chunks so you don't have to keep the entire game design in your head at once.

Procedures thus play a pivotal role in Logo programming. The design of versatile procedures is a craft we will explore in this book. One of the programming tools that can make procedures extremely versatile is *recursion*.

The Power of Recursion

The concept of recursion and recursive programming is probably one of the most difficult ideas in computer programming. Were it not such a useful and powerful tool, I would be tempted to ignore it. But as fate would have it, recursion is a tool that, once understood, allows us to formulate programmed solutions to problems far easier than you would have ever imagined, so you should probably make some effort to master it.

Technically, a procedure is recursive when part of its definition uses the procedure itself. At this level, recursion sounds insane—somewhat like picking yourself up by your own bootstraps. Of course, the reason you can't pick yourself up by your bootstraps (or sandal thongs, if you prefer) is because that is an all-at-once activity. Computational procedures (in the computers we use, anyway) operate serially, one command at a time. This serial nature of the computation overcomes the all-at-onceness problem.

Even if we think in stepwise terms, we can still be confused by recursion. For example, we sometimes encounter recursion in puzzles such as:

A town has only one barber. The barber shaves everyone who doesn't shave himself. Who shaves the barber?

If we start thinking about this problem, we encounter a paradox. The barber shaves himself only if he doesn't shave himself. We can stay stuck in this loop until we give up or decide that the barber is a woman who doesn't need to be shaved!

From a computational perspective, recursion is sometimes introduced in the following manner. We start with a procedure to draw a few lines on the screen. For example:

```
TO SHAPE
FD 40 RT 150 FD 60
END
```

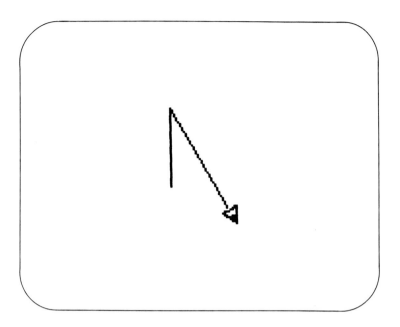

Each time the name of this procedure is typed into the computer, these two lines are drawn on the screen, with each new set starting at the ending point of the previous set. This procedure can be made recursive by modifying it to have the following form:

```
TO SHAPE
FD 40 RT 150 FD 60
SHAPE
END
```

This version of the procedure is similar to the first, except that the procedure name is included after the commands to draw the lines. This is an example of *tail-end* recursion. If we now enter

```
SHAPE
```

a complete pattern will be drawn on the screen, and the turtle will continue to trace this pattern indefinitely. To stop the turtle, hold down the open apple key and press the esc key.

In this example, recursion was used to simulate the repetition of a set of commands indefinitely. Notice that I used the word *simulate*, because these commands were not being repeated in the ordinary sense of the word. This is where recursion can be tricky to understand.

In analyzing how this procedure works, we can start by looking at other ways to produce this figure on the screen. One way to do this in Logo is with the **REPEAT** command. For example:

REPEAT 12 [FD 40 RT 150 FD 60]

produces the same figure on the screen. In this case, the commands **FD 40 RT 150 FD 60** are being repeated 12 times. This type of repetition is called a *loop*. Looping is not recursive!

If you are familiar with BASIC, you may be tempted to compare our recursive procedure with a loop using the GOTO statement, such as:

```
10 REM THIS IS THE START OF THE LOOP
20 PRINT "This sentence will be printed forever."
30 GOTO 10
40 END
```

In this case, the GOTO statement in line 30 causes the program to branch back to line 10. As with our recursive procedure, this loop will run indefinitely, but even this BASIC example is not recursive.

To see just what recursion is, we can examine the execution of our procedure line by line. When we first type the procedure name, it encounters instructions to draw two lines, which are then drawn on the screen.

```
  TO SHAPE
• FD 40 RT 150 FD 60
  SHAPE
  END
```

(The bullet mark (•) shows the commands being executed when the lines are drawn.)

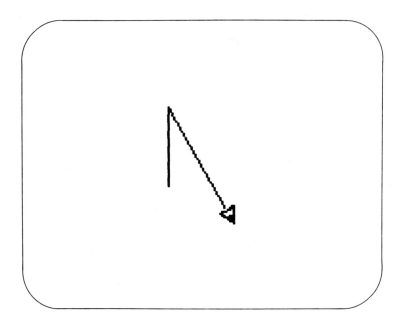

Next, Logo comes to the command **SHAPE**. As we said before, Logo interprets any word as an instruction to be run. So when Logo encounters **SHAPE** it runs a copy of this procedure. Structurally, we can think of the procedure:

```
TO SHAPE
FD 40 RT 150 FD 60
SHAPE
END
```

being rewritten the following way after encountering the word **SHAPE** for the first time:

```
TO SHAPE
FD 40 RT 150 FD 60
•      FD 40 RT 150 FD 60
       SHAPE
       END
END
```

The bullet is shown at the next line to be executed. When this copy is run, we see two more lines drawn on the screen:

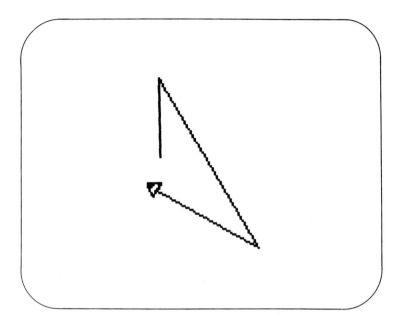

Next, Logo encounters the word **SHAPE** again and runs another copy of this procedure. We can write this new copy into our original this way:

```
TO SHAPE
FD 40 RT 150 FD 60
      FD 40 RT 150 FD 60
●            FD 40 RT 150 FD 60
             SHAPE
             END
         END
END
```

As in the previous examples, the bullet shows which line is to be executed next.

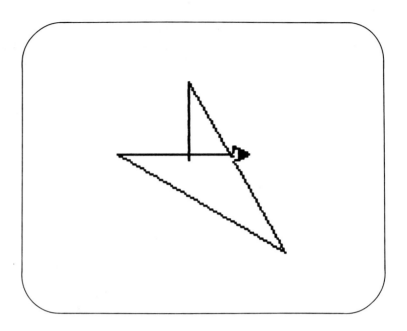

A recursive procedure makes copies of itself each time it encounters its own name. The internal bookkeeping that keeps these copies separate from each other assigns each copy to its own "level." Every time a procedure uses another procedure, the new procedure operates at a new level inside Logo. When a procedure finishes its execution (either by coming to an **END** command or a **STOP** command), it then transfers control back to the procedure that called it in the first place.

In our example there is no way for the procedures to ever end, because each new copy of **SHAPE** includes an instruction to run an even newer copy of **SHAPE**. Logo patiently keeps track of these copies until it starts to run out of memory. At that point, Logo automatically runs a "garbage-collection" procedure that cleans up the workspace before continuing. Because the next command after the word **SHAPE** is **END**, Logo really doesn't need to keep track of all the different copies of **SHAPE**, and the garbage collector can recover lots of computer memory for the system to use.

To see one more example of tail-end recursion, enter the following procedure:

```
TO COUNTER :number
PRINT :number
COUNTER :number + 1
END
```

If we now enter a command like the following,

```
TEXTSCREEN
COUNTER 1
```

we will see a column of numbers appear on the screen:

```
1
2
3
4
5
6
7
.

.

.
```

This is another example of a tail-end recursive procedure that will continue until we stop it. To see how it works, notice that the first command prints the contents of the local variable **number** on the screen. Next, it encounters a command to use the procedure **COUNTER** with a number given by the old number (1) plus 1. Because local variables are not only local to their procedures but are also local to the level or copy of the procedure being used, there is no confusion about what value should be used when the copy of **COUNTER** is executed. Similarly, when the copy of **COUNTER** runs its copy, the new variable will be set to the value of the old variable (2) plus 1.

To see how Logo handles this procedure, we will make a

change in it. This change will cause the procedure to stop when the value for number equals 10.

```
TO COUNTER :number
IF EQUALP :number 10 [STOP]
PRINT :number
COUNTER :number + 1
END
```

The new line we added uses the **IF** command, which tests the truthfulness of a predicate (in our case, the equality of the value of number and 10). If the predicate is **TRUE**, then the commands in the list following the predicate are executed. Otherwise the commands are not executed, and Logo moves to the next line of commands. (Later we will use another form of the **IF** command, which will be described at that time.)

To see how this version of **COUNTER** works, we can enter:

TRACE "COUNTER

This command causes Logo to show us a trace of **COUNTER**'s execution. This trace illustrates the recursive nature of counter very nicely. If we now enter

COUNTER 1

the screen will show:

```
COUNTER 1
1
  COUNTER 2
2
    COUNTER 3
3
      COUNTER 4
4
        COUNTER 5
5
          COUNTER 6
6
            COUNTER 7
7
              COUNTER 8
8
                COUNTER 9
9
                  COUNTER 10
                  COUNTER stopped
                COUNTER stopped
              COUNTER stopped
            COUNTER stopped
          COUNTER stopped
        COUNTER stopped
      COUNTER stopped
    COUNTER stopped
  COUNTER stopped
COUNTER stopped
```

The **TRACE** command causes each procedure call to appear on the screen. The "nesting" shows that **COUNTER 1** results in the calling of **COUNTER 2** and so on. Each time a copy of **COUNTER** is executed, its local value for number is compared with the value 10. As soon as a copy of **COUNTER** uses the value **10**, the Logo command **STOP** is executed. **STOP** returns Logo to the procedure that called the one that just stopped. The return point is the command that follows the one that finished. The command that finished was **COUNTER 10**, and the command after that is the END command in COUNTER 9. This finishes COUNTER 9, and Logo then goes to COUNTER 8 where it again encounters END, and so on until Logo returns to the top level, which is the level at which you type your commands to Logo.

The TRACE command is a valuable tool for tracking the levels of recursion in your Logo procedures. To stop the trace, just enter:

UNTRACE "COUNTER

A more graphic example of this type of recursion appears in the following cartoon by Larry Wright.

KIT 'N' CARLYLE™   by Larry Wright

© 1982 Newspaper Enterprise Association, Inc.

This cartoon shows:

A cat dreaming about
     a cat dreaming about
          a cat dreaming about
               a cat dreaming about
                    a cat eating.

Fortunately for the cat, his recursive dream cycle had a STOP command at the eating dream, or he would be lost in sleep forever!

Before exploring other types of recursion, I will describe one more example: that of "squiral" (square spiral) curves. The pictures generated by the procedure we create have become synonymous with turtle graphics, so we might as well include them for old-time's sake. The idea behind these figures is that we will create a figure by drawing a line, turning by some angle, drawing a line longer than the first line, and repeating this process until the lines reach a preset limit.

This type of figure can be created with nonrecursive procedures, but it is instructive to see the recursive version in action:


```
TO SQUIRAL :size :angle
IF :size > 100 [STOP]
FD :size RT :angle
SQUIRAL :size + 1 :angle
END
```


To see some figures produced by this procedure we can enter


```
CS SQUIRAL 1 91
```


or

CS SQUIRAL 1 143

or experiment with values of our own.

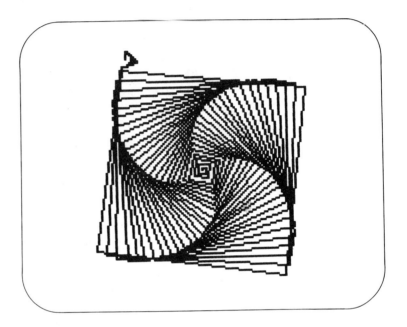

By now you probably understand how this procedure works. After drawing each line, a new copy of **SQUIRAL** is run with a slightly larger value for the line length. We can see this procedure in action by first setting it to operate one step at a time. This is done with the Logo **STEP** command:

```
STEP "SQUIRAL
```

This command causes **SQUIRAL** to operate one step at a time. For example, we can enter:

```
CS SQUIRAL 50 91
```

As we press the return key over and over again, this procedure advances to the next step of its execution. We will see each line being drawn on the screen and also a listing of the actions taken by the computer at each step:

```
SQUIRAL 50 91
IF :size > 100 [STOP]
FD :size RT :angle
SQUIRAL :size + 1 :angle
IF :size > 100 [STOP]
FD :size RT :angle
SQUIRAL :size + 1 :angle
```

To clear the **STEP** function, enter:

```
UNSTEP "SQUIRAL
```

So far we have been exploring tail-end recursion. Now it is time to explore another form of this powerful tool: *embedded recursion*.

The primary difference between embedded recursion and tail-end recursion is that procedures with embedded recursion have more tasks to perform as each lower level of the procedure finishes its task. For a simple example, let's start with our previously defined procedure called COUNTER:

```
TO COUNTER :number
IF EQUALP :number 10 [STOP]
PRINT :number
COUNTER :number + 1
END
```

When we entered

```
COUNTER 1
```

we saw a list of numbers on the screen ranging from 1 to 9. Next, we can modify COUNTER so it looks like this:

```
TO COUNTER :number
IF EQUALP :number 10 [STOP]
PRINT :number
COUNTER :number + 1
PRINT :number
END
```

Before using this procedure, see if you can predict what it will do.

Now enter:

```
COUNTER 1
```

to see what happens. The screen should now display the following:

```
1
2
3
4
5
6
7
8
9
9
8
7
6
5
4
3
2
1
```

This procedure prints the numbers from 1 to 9 and then prints the numbers from 9 to 1. We can use the **STEP** or **TRACE** commands to see this procedure in action. Our modified version of **COUNTER** uses embedded recursion. Procedures that use embedded recursion have tasks to perform after the recursive part is finished. In our example, when **COUNTER** tried to use a value of number equal to **10**, the predicate (**EQUALP** :number 10) became true and the tenth level of **COUNTER** executed a **STOP** command. This returned us to the second **PRINT** statement in the ninth level of **COUNTER**. Once this command was carried out, the **END** statement terminated the ninth level of **COUNTER** and returned us to the second **PRINT** command in the eighth level of **COUNTER**. This process was repeated until the first level of **COUNTER** finished its tasks and returned us to the top level of Logo. *Whew!*

Embedded recursion can accomplish great things with short programs, but it takes some effort to understand it.

For a graphic example of embedded recursion, we can

make a modified SQUIRAL procedure to show a connected pair of "squiral" curves. We can edit SQUIRAL to have a smaller limit (to keep our picture on the screen) and to draw some more lines after the recursive portion of the definition:

```
TO SQUIRAL :size :angle
IF :size > 89 [STOP]
FD :size RT :angle
SQUIRAL :size + 1 :angle
FD :size LT :angle
END
```

If we now enter

```
CS SQUIRAL 1 91
```

we will see this figure on the screen:

The "squiral" on the left was drawn by the commands *before* the recursive statement, and the "squiral" on the right was drawn by the commands *after* the recursive statement. As this figure was being drawn, you probably noticed that the first "squiral" was drawn with lines that got progressively longer and the second "squiral" was drawn with lines that got progressively shorter. If you are still having a hard time understanding why this is the case, you might want to reexamine COUNTER.

Because by definition only the END command can follow the recursive statement in tail-end recursion, this form is limited to one recursive statement per procedure. There is no limit, however, to the number of recursive statements that can be used with embedded recursion. In fact, this characteristic is used to great advantage in creating trees and fractal curves.

To create a procedure to draw a tree, consider the shape shown in the following figure:

This figure shows a branching pattern reminiscent. To see how we might define a procedure to draw this shape, let's start with the turtle at the base of the tree. First we need to turn the turtle to the left by an angle to point it along the left branch. If we were drawing only two branches we would move the turtle forward by the branch length, move it back, turn it to the right, and repeat the drawing of the right branch. For one pair of branches we might write:

```
TO TREE :size :angle
LT :angle
FD :size
BK :size
RT :angle * 2
FD :size
BK :size
LT :angle
END
```

If we try this procedure by entering

```
TREE 45 45
```

we will see that it draws two branches and leaves the turtle at its starting state.

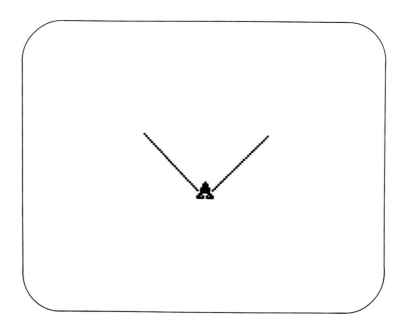

Of course, the problem with this version of the tree is that it draws only two branches and then stops. To make a more interesting tree we need to look at our original pattern again. If you look at the tree you will see that a new pair of branches is drawn at the end of each longer branch. This process continues until the branch size becomes smaller than a predetermined amount. The following modified version of **TREE** does this for us:

```
TO TREE :size :angle
IF :size < 2 [STOP]
LT :angle
FD :size
TREE :size / 1.61803 :angle
BK :size
RT :angle * 2
FD :size
TREE :size / 1.61803 :angle
BK :size
LT :angle
END
```

(Our use of 1.61803 as the divisor is arbitrary, but it does give us a pretty tree. The fact that 1.61803 is an approximation of the golden mean is significant and is described in *Discovering Apple Logo*.)

Try drawing trees with different angles; the patterns can be quite nice. For example, the following figures were created by typing:

CS TREE 40 30
CS TREE 45 45

and

CS TREE 45 60

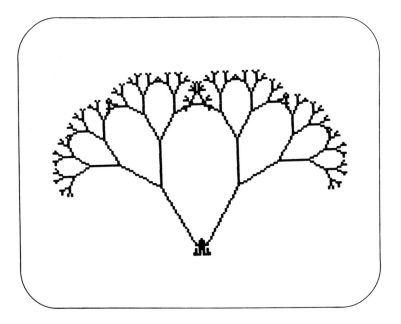

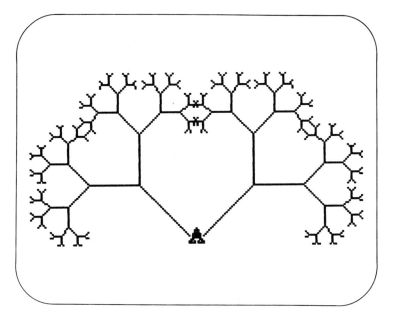

You may have noticed that these trees took a while to draw. We can speed up the process by hiding the turtle before running the procedure. Quite simply, there is a "whole lot of computin'" going on in these recursive procedures. Because these complex trees are being drawn with a procedure 12 lines long, you can see why recursion is a boon to the programmer.

As one last graphic example of embedded recursion I will touch on the topic of fractal geometry—the branch of mathematics that, among other things, gave us the realistic computer-generated landscapes in the movie *Star Trek II: The Wrath of Khan*.

For our example, we will start with a simple shape—a line with a triangular bump in its center:

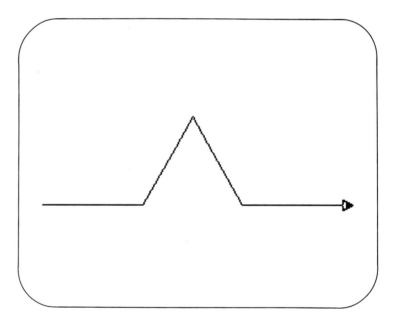

Next, we will replace each straight-line segment with a suitably reduced copy of the original figure:

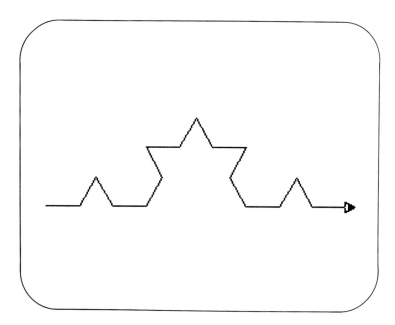

The curve we want to create results from the continued replacement of straight lines by copies of the original shape, until the copies are smaller than a predetermined limit:

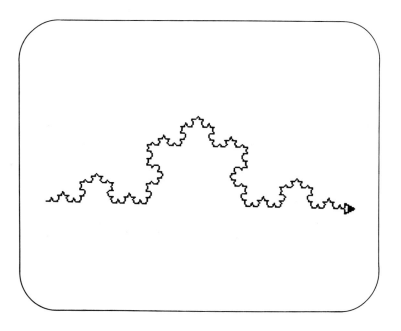

Because this curve was discovered by the mathematician H. von Koch, its procedure is named after him. To start, we need a procedure to set the turtle at the left side of the screen and to point the turtle to the right:

```
TO SETUP :pos
PU SETPOS :pos SETHEADING 90 PD
END
```

Next, we can draw the first shape with a simple procedure:

```
TO K1 :size
FD :size
LT 60
FD :size
RT 120
FD :size
LT 60
FD :size
END
```

If we now enter:

```
CS SETUP [−120 −60] K1 81
```

we will see the first curve on the screen. The problem with K1, however, is that it lets us create only the first level. In fact, we want to have a version of K1 executed in place of each straight line until the line length is reduced below a chosen limit. The following procedure does this for us:

```
TO KOCH :size :limit
IF :size < :limit [FD :size STOP]
KOCH :size / 3 :limit
LT 60
KOCH :size / 3 :limit
RT 120
KOCH :size / 3 :limit
LT 60
KOCH :size / 3 :limit
END
```

Because each line segment is one-third of the horizontal distance of the pattern, we must divide the line length by 3 for each successive level of the curve. To generate the figures shown before, we should enter:

```
CS SETUP [−120 −60] KOCH 243 243
CS SETUP [−120 −60] KOCH 243 81
```

and

```
CS SETUP [−120 −60] KOCH 243 9
```

The reasons we used 243 as the starting size are that it is a power of 3 and that the first accepted value for drawing lines (81) gives us a figure that fits nicely on the display screen.

These curves are easy to experiment with on our own. For example, we can build a fractal snowflake by entering:

```
CS REPEAT 3 [KOCH 81 9 RT 120]
```

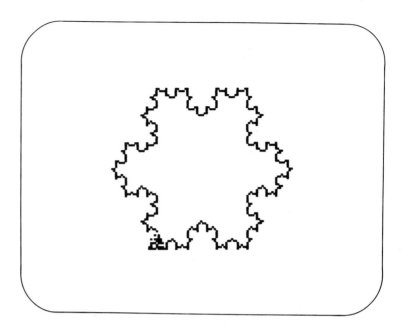

The mathematics behind these curves is described in *Discovering Apple Logo*, so, as fascinating as it is, I will resist the temptation to elaborate further on this topic by sending you to that reference and to the digression on fractals in appendix 2.

Our next task is to explore Logo's ability to compute with numbers.

IV.

Computing with Numbers

At last we are ready to explore a domain many people think is at the heart of computer use: numbers. In fact, non-numerical programming is fast becoming the rule rather than the exception, but numbers will always have their place. Accordingly, Logo comes well equipped to handle numeric information.

Introducing Logo's Numbers and Simple Operations

There are two types of numbers that Logo uses: *integers* and *decimals*. Both kinds are expressed in base 10 (i.e., they are composed of the numerals 0 through 9), although numbers in other bases can also be created. One way that distinguishes the computer's use of numbers from our own is the concept of a limit. There is no limit to the size of numbers we can think about or use. But because Logo allocates 32 bits of data to each number, integers are limited to the range from 2,147,483,647 to $-2,147,483,648$, and decimals can have six digits of accuracy and can include an exponent that ranges from 10^{38} to 10^{-37}.

The following numbers are integers:

3141567   0 -27

The following numbers are decimals:

6.   45.3675   3.5E10   4.5N27

The appearance of a decimal point tells us we are using decimal numbers. Numbers that require more than six digits to express are written in what is called scientific notation. The number **3.5E10** is 3.5 times 10^{10}. The number **4.5N27** is 4.5

times 10^{-27}. The letter **E** means the exponent is positive, and **N** means it is negative.

Some Logo operations work only with integers, and others work only with decimals. If these operations are given the wrong type of number, Logo performs the transformation to the correct form automatically and expresses the result in this new form.

To perform a computation in Logo, we must write an expression. For example:

PRINT SUM 9 37.1

This will cause the result (46.1) to be printed on the screen. Notice that the result is a decimal, even though the numbers to be added were an integer (9) and a decimal (37.1).

The four traditional arithmetic operators include SUM, DIF-FERENCE, PRODUCT, and QUOTIENT. Each of these operations expects two inputs. For example,

PRINT SUM 48 4

produces 52;

PRINT DIFFERENCE 48 4

produces 44;

PRINT PRODUCT 48 4

produces 192; and

PRINT QUOTIENT 48 4

produces 12.0. QUOTIENT always produces a decimal result, even if the inputs are integers. We will soon see another form of QUOTIENT that always produces integers, regardless of the form of the input numbers.

The operations I have shown thus far are all in the traditional Logo prefix form. However, to make life easy for people who use calculators, Logo also contains a set of *infix* operators:

3 + 5 is equivalent to SUM 3 5
3 − 5 is equivalent to DIFFERENCE 3 5
3 * 5 is equivalent to PRODUCT 3 5
3 / 5 is equivalent to QUOTIENT 3 5

Because you are most likely familiar with infix notation for arithmetic, use these forms if they are comfortable for you, and ignore the fact that they deviate from Logo's prefix style.

When working with Logo's arithmetic operations, continue to exercise caution in your use of spaces. In particular, you must place a space between each item in an expression, as with other Logo expressions. For example,

PRINT 12 / 6

produces 2.0; and

PRINT 12/6

produces

I DON'T KNOW HOW TO 12/6

There are some exceptions to this rule, but it is better to be safe than sorry, so always be sure to leave spaces between items in your expressions.

One reason this rule is important is that it lets us express negative numbers by placing the minus sign immediately before the number. For example,

MAKE "RESULT −78

stores −78 in the variable named RESULT. As it turns out, you can insert a space between the minus and the 78 without affecting the result for this example, but it is generally a good idea to use spaces to distinguish between subtraction (use a space) and the unary minus command (no space).

When Logo evaluates math commands, it evaluates them in a particular precedence rather than simply from left to right. The normal precedence for the operations we described is (from highest to lowest); unary minus (minus sign with no space); multiplication and division using * and /; addition and subtraction using + and −; and all other operations including SUM, DIFFERENCE, the other Logo primitive math operations, and those we create on our own.

Of course we may not want operations performed in this sequence and instead want to use a computational precedence of our own. Logo lets us do this through the use of parentheses. For example, if we enter

PRINT 2 * 3 + 4 / 5

we will get 6.8; if we enter

PRINT 2 * (3 + 4 / 5)

we will get 7.6; and if we enter

PRINT 2 * (3 + 4) / 5

we will get 2.8. When you are not absolutely sure of the sequence in which your computations will be performed, be sure to use parentheses to cluster operations in the desired sequences.

Logo Integer Operations

There are times when decimal numbers are simply not appropriate. For example, I heard of a doctor who had a patient come to him with the following complaint:

"Doc, I think I've got a touch of the pregnancy!"

Yes, there are some things that just are (or just aren't), and integers play an important role when talking about these things. It is one thing to say that, over the entire poplulation, there are 2.3 children per household, and another to say that Ron deRonchegos is an average father, so *he* has 2.3 children. Children come in whole numbers, rocks come in whole numbers, ice cubes come in whole numbers. Logo has some whole-number tools. Two of these are devoted to transforming decimals to integers. The first of these is the INT operation, which strips off the decimal part of the number and returns the integer part. For example,

PRINT INT 3.1

gives 3, and

PRINT INT 0.9999

gives 0.

INT seems hardly fair in its truncation process. After all, 0.9999 is pretty close to 1, so why should we get 0? For those concerned with fairness in integers, Logo has a special operation called ROUND. This operation returns the integer closest to the decimal number it is converting. For example,

PRINT ROUND 3.1

gives 3,

PRINT ROUND 6.5

gives 7, and

PRINT ROUND −12.8

gives −13.

ROUND behaves much more sensibly than INT for some types of computations, and we must choose between these two commands carefully.

For example, suppose your bank-account interest is compounded daily. If you have an account that yields 10.65% interest per year, and your starting balance is $1265.96, your first day's interest will be 1265.96 × 0.1065 /365, or $0.36938284932. Now, your bank officials might say to themselves, "What the heck, we can't keep track of fractional cents, so we'll give this account 36 cents interest today." Of course, they might decide to keep the $0.00938284932 amount in the bank's own account (to be certain that its internal books will balance, of course), and this amount would be added to the similar remainders from the other accounts. Of course, if they did that, and the bank had 25,000 customers, it might accumulate a few hundred dollars per day as pure gravy. This would only amount to, say, $85,000 a year that nobody would ever miss. Now, this sum would only be the amount collected by a small bank. A large bank might produce quite a bit more than that. This is all purely hypothetical, of course; after all, if banks really did things like this they would be able to afford marble façades and plush leather chairs and all that sort of stuff.

So, you see that a knowledge of the "proper" use of INT could be quite profitable!

Two other Logo integer operations can come in quite handy: INTQUOTIENT and REMAINDER. You may recall that QUOTIENT produced a decimal result. By using INTQUOTIENT and REMAINDER we can perform division the way we used to do it in grammar school: "Seven divided by three is two with a remainder of one." Note two things about this answer: first, it is expressed entirely in integers; second, unlike its decimal counterpart, it is accurate. The decimal result, 2.3333, is not accurate, because the 3s have to continue forever. Even if we say the answer is 2.3333333333333333333333333333333333333333333 we still won't be accurate (even though we will be mighty close). Some numbers simply can't be expressed as decimals.

To see how these operations work, note that if we enter

PRINT INTQUOTIENT 12 6

we will get 2 and that if we enter

PRINT INTQUOTIENT 1 3

we will get 0. INTQUOTIENT produces the whole-number part of the division as its result. The REMAINDER operation produces only the part that is left over when the division is finished. For example,

PRINT REMAINDER 10 3

produces 1, because that is the amount left over when 10 is divided by 3. We can explore INTQUOTIENT and REMAINDER in a small procedure that converts minutes into hours and minutes:

```
TO CONVERT :mins
PRINT (SENTENCE INTQUOTIENT :mins 60 [hours and]
     REMAINDER :mins 60 [minutes])
END
```

(If you don't already know what **SENTENCE** does, don't worry about it—it is described in the next chapter. (It will also explain our use of the parentheses in this procedure. (Parenthetically, parentheses are one of the characteristic attributes of LISP programs, and one can tell when a LISP procedure is finished by looking for all the closing parentheses. (In general, this is not a characteristic of Logo, however.))))

This procedure takes the starting number of minutes (mins) and produces the integer number of hours (using **INTQUOTIENT**) and the number of remaining minutes (using **REMAINDER**). For example,

CONVERT 3600

produces

60 hours and 0 minutes

and

CONVERT 125

produces

2 hours and 5 minutes

"Mathaholics" will notice that the **REMAINDER** operation is also the same as the "modulo" operation. Because you may not be absolutely entranced with the properties of modular arithmetic, I will restrain myself from further elaboration on this topic.

Special Decimal Operations

In addition to the operations that have already been described, Logo provides several transcendental operations. In mathematics, a function is transcendental when it cannot be expressed in a finite algebraic expression.

The functions with which Logo comes equipped include the trigonometric functions SIN, COS, and ARCTAN and the ever-popular square root (SQRT). In the case of SIN and COS, these operations produce the sine and cosine of an angle expressed in degrees. ARCTAN converts a tangent into an angle between 90 and −90 degrees. One of the nice properties of trigonometry is that once we have SIN, COS, and ARCTAN (and SQRT), we can generate the other trigonometric functions such as TAN, ARCSIN, and ARCCOS:

```
TO TAN :ang
IF EQUALP COS :ang 0 [OUTPUT 0] [OUTPUT
    (SIN :ang) / (COS :ang)]
END

TO ARCSIN :×
IF EQUALP ABS :× 1 [OUTPUT 90] [OUTPUT ARCTAN :× /
    (SQRT 1 − :× * :×)]
END

TO ARCCOS :×
IF EQUALP :× 0 [OUTPUT 90] [OUTPUT ARCTAN
    (SQRT 1 − :× * :×) / :×]
END
```

The ARCSIN procedure uses another procedure that finds the absolute value of a number:

```
TO ABS :×
IF :× < 0 [OUTPUT −:×] [OUTPUT :×]
END
```

Notice that all three of our operations have been protected against division by zero. This is the function of the **IF** statement in each definition. Logo is not particularly fond of division by zero, because it tends to produce unwieldy numbers.

To see what these functions look like we can plot them on the screen. To do this we must first create a set of axes on the screen and then plot each function after setting the initial plotting position and value. For example, we could use the following procedure:

```
TO PLOT.OPERS
CS HIDETURTLE
DRAW.AXES
PLOT.START SIN.PLOT 0
PLOT.START COS.PLOT 0
PLOT.START TAN.PLOT 0
END
```

The axes are drawn with the procedure **DRAW.AXES**:

```
TO DRAW.AXES
PU SETPOS [-135 -75]PD
REPEAT 2 [FD 180 RT 90 FD 270 RT 90]
REPEAT 7 [FD 25 RT 90 FD 5 BK 10 FD 5 LT 90]
BK 175
END
```

When this procedure is run it produces the following figure.

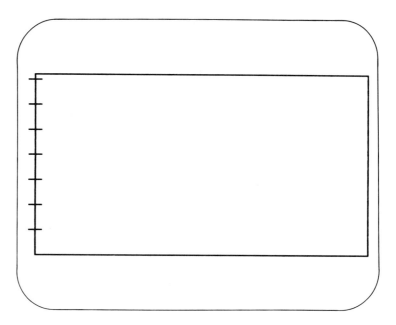

Next, PLOT.START sets the starting position for the plot and sets the value of the global variable, START:

```
TO PLOT.START
PU SETPOS [-135 0] PD
MAKE "START -135
END
```

We now need procedures that plot the sine, cosine, and tangent functions:

```
TO SIN.PLOT :ang
IF :ang > 250 [STOP]
SETPOS SENTENCE :START + :ang 75 * SIN (:ang * 2)
SIN.PLOT :ang + 1
END
```

```
TO COS.PLOT :ang
IF :ang > 250 [STOP]
SETPOS SENTENCE :START + :ang 75 * COS (:ang * 2)
COS.PLOT :ang + 1
END

TO TAN.PLOT :ang
IF :ang > 250 [STOP]
SETPOS SENTENCE :START + :ang 5 * TAN (:ang * 2)
TAN.PLOT :ang + 1
END
```

Notice that we multiply :ang by 2 in each operation. This plots the curves in two-degree increments and lets all three of these procedures plot values for angles up to 500 degrees. Each of them has been scaled to fit nicely on the screen. Because TAN can produce very large numbers, we have used a much smaller scale factor for TAN (5) than we did for SIN and COS (75).

If we now enter

PLOT.OPERS

we will see three curves drawn on our set of axes, one at a time:

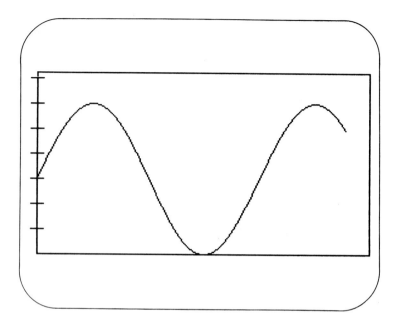

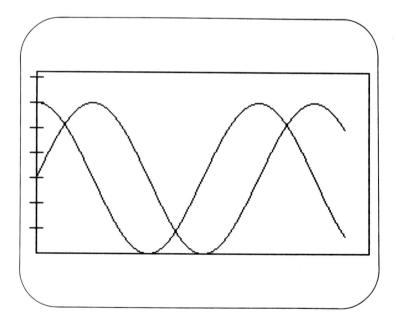

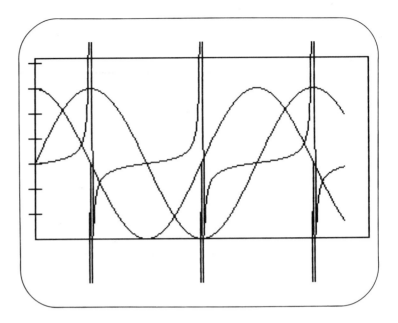

The only difference between the sine and cosine curves is a phase shift of 90 degrees. At an angle of zero degrees, the value of SIN is 0 and that of COS is 1. The behavior of TAN (shown in above figure) is far more exciting because as COS approaches zero, the magnitude of TAN grows without bound. But as the angle passes through 90 degrees, TAN goes from $+\infty$ to $-\infty$. To make TAN behave better at this point, we set its value to 0 when the value of COS reaches 0 (at 90 degrees, for example). The TAN function resembles the pattern of a heartbeat.

The SQRT operation is not nearly as exciting as the others mentioned. Its task is simply to give the square root of any positive number it is given. For example,

PRINT SQRT 56

gives 7.48331. Some applications for SQRT are described later.

Random Numbers

Normally, we tell Logo what numbers we want to work with. If we want Logo to add two numbers, we must specify which numbers it is to add. If we want to take a square root (and who doesn't these days), we must tell Logo which number to take the square root of.

Well, if we run out of numbers of our own, Logo has an operation that will produce numbers for us. The numbers Logo picks are "randomly" chosen using the RANDOM operation. The reason for placing the word randomly in quotes is that Logo's numbers aren't truly random. In fact, we can replay a set of numbers by using the RERANDOM command.

RANDOM produces integers between 0 and one less than the number specified. For example,

PRINT RANDOM 100

will print a number between 0 and 99. To see some of Logo's random numbers, enter the following:

REPEAT 10 [PRINT RANDOM 10]

When I did this, the following numbers appeared on the screen:

1
8
3
8
1
2
5
1
6
1

There are lots of practical applications for random numbers, but we tend to encounter them mostly in games of chance. Whether it is a simple matter of flipping a coin, rolling a pair of dice, or shuffling a deck of cards, randomness plays an important role.

Let's start with one of the most lucrative myths in the field of random numbers: the so-called Law of Averages. There is no such thing as the Law of Averages, as the wealth of the Las Vegas casinos can attest. But even so, gamblers the whole world over seem to think their luck will turn because of some divine balance predicted by this "law." To get a flavor for what we are talking about, let's build a coin flipper in Logo:

```
TO FLIP
OUTPUT IF EQUALP RANDOM 2 1 ["HEADS] ["TAILS]
END
```

Notice that we have written this procedure so we need to type **OUTPUT** only once. If this obfuscates things for you, feel free to use instead:

```
IF EQUALP RANDOM 2 1 [OUTPUT "HEADS] [OUTPUT "TAILS]
```

Because **RANDOM 2** can have one of only two values (0 and 1), it is equally likely for the word **HEADS** to be chosen as it is for **TAILS** to be chosen.

Now, step right up folks—don't crowd the computer—we're going to do a little experiment. If we enter

```
REPEAT 15 [PRINT FLIP]
```

we might get the following result:

HEADS
TAILS
HEADS
HEADS
TAILS
TAILS
TAILS
TAILS
HEADS
HEADS
HEADS
HEADS
HEADS
HEADS
HEADS

Notice that out of 15 flips, I got 5 **TAILS** and 10 **HEADS**. Now, here's your chance to win it all—just tell me the likelihood of the next flip producing a **TAIL**. If you believed in the Law of Averages, you would say, "Hey, heads have been out-numbering tails by 2 to 1, and on the average things have to balance out, so I'll guess that it is more likely for **TAILS** to come up this time."

The casinos would surely like you to think that, because the fact of the matter is that the likelihood of **HEADS** or **TAILS** is still the same at each flip of the coin. After all, if the coin is perfectly balanced there is no reason for one side to be favored over the other. This is true if the previous 100 flips produced **HEADS** or even if the previous 10,000 flips produced **HEADS**. Although it is very unlikely that this would happen (in fact, the likelihood is $0.5^{10,000}$), it *is* possible. And if you think about it, the coin hasn't the foggiest notion which side it has been landing on, so how could it influence its next position?

Of course, this doesn't keep people from speaking to their dice or to the roulette wheel. The Law of Averages has another name—the Monte Carlo Fallacy.

Even so, we can make predictions about the behavior of random numbers; we can always figure the odds or likelihood of a particular event occurring. For example, if we throw a pair of six-sided dice and add the face values together, we will get one of eleven numbers from 2 to 12. Now let's say someone made a perfectly balanced 11-sided die (a very tricky proposition), and the faces were numbered from 2 to 12. The question is: If we needed to throw a 7 and had the choice of throwing the two six-sided dice and adding them together or throwing the 11-sided die, which would be the better choice? For the 11-sided die, the likelihood of any face landing up is the same—1 out of 11. For the two six-sided dice the likelihood of any number coming up is 1 out of 6, which gives a combined probability of 1 out of 36 for both dice. But we must be careful here, because there are several ways to get a 7 with two dice. We can throw any of the following combinations:

1 and 6,
2 and 5,
3 and 4,
4 and 3,
5 and 2,
6 and 1

This gives us six combinations for a 7, for a total likelihood of 6 out of 36 (or 1 out of 6). As a result, we would be better off rolling the two dice for a 7. If, however, we wanted to roll a 2, we would be better off with the 11-sided die (1 out of 11) than with the two six-sided dice (1 out of 36). Of course, this just refers to the likelihoods, not to realities. It is possible (but not likely) for someone to throw a 2 ten times in a row.

We can build a Logo model of our dice-throwing world and then examine our results. The method for doing this involves a list of variables, each of which is named by a number between 2 and 12. If you don't follow all of the list activities in this section, don't worry, they are explained in the next chapter.

To start, we can make a model for the throwing of our 11-sided die:

```
TO THROW11
LOCAL "value
MAKE "value (2 + RANDOM 11)
MAKE :value 1 + THING :value
END
```

What, you might ask, am I doing in this procedure? It assumes that I have created 11 variables whose names are **2, 3, 4, 5, . . ., 12**. Each of these variables will start out with a contents of zero. Each time THROW11 is used, one of these variable names is chosen randomly and assigned to the local variable, **value**, with the line:

```
MAKE "value (2 + RANDOM 11)
```

(Notice that we declared **value** to be local with the **LOCAL** command. If we hadn't done this, **value** would have been created as a global variable, and this might have accidentally interfered with the operation of some other procedures. In general, you will find your programming life will be much smoother if you define global variables only when you are sure that you want the same variables to be accessed by any of several procedures.) Next, the contents of this variable is increased by 1 with the line:

```
MAKE :value 1 + THING :value
```

To use this procedure, we must first initialize the variables. For convenience, we can store the variable names in a list:

```
MAKE "DICE [2 3 4 5 6 7 8 9 10 11 12]
```

We can set the values of these variables to zero with the recursive procedure:

```
TO INIT :list
IF EMPTYP :list [STOP]
MAKE FIRST :list 0
INIT BUTFIRST :list
END
```

(Again, we are just looking for results here. The operation of procedures like this is explained in the next chapter.)

To initialize the variables, enter:

INIT :DICE

If we now test the contents of the variables by entering

PRINT :2

etc., we will see that they each have the value 0. Next, we should "throw" our die a few times to see how frequently the various numbers appear. For example, if we enter

REPEAT 1100 [THROW11]

we will simulate the throwing of this die 1100 times. This will take Logo a little over a minute to do, so be patient. Next, we can see the result of our throws with the following recursive procedure:

```
TO RESULTS :list
IF EMPTYP :list [STOP]
PRINT (SENTENCE FIRST :list [came up] THING FIRST :list
    [times])
RESULTS BUTFIRST :list
END
```

Because we threw the die 1100 times, and the probability for each face is the same (1 out of 11), we expect that each face of the die should have come up 100 times. To see the result of the experiment, enter:

RESULT :DICE

The results I obtained are shown here:

2 came up 74 times
3 came up 119 times
4 came up 114 times
5 came up 97 times
6 came up 93 times
7 came up 107 times
8 came up 87 times
9 came up 96 times
10 came up 102 times
11 came up 99 times
12 came up 112 times

Next, let's explore the results from throwing two six-sided dice. We can modify **THROW11** as shown below:

```
TO THROW2
LOCAL :value
MAKE "value (1 + RANDOM 6) + (1 + RANDOM 6)
MAKE :value 1 + THING :value
END
```

The only difference between **THROW11** and **THROW2** is that we have replaced

2 + RANDOM 11

with

(1 + RANDOM 6) + (1 + RANDOM 6)

As we shall soon see, these lines are *not* equivalent. The first computation represents the throwing of one die, and the second is the combined action of throwing two dice. To see our new result, enter:

```
INIT :DICE
REPEAT 1100 [THROW2]
RESULTS :DICE
```

Rather than the uniform distribution of numbers we saw for our single die, we now get a very nonuniform distribution of numbers. On the basis of strict probabilities, the numbers 2 and 12 should only appear 1/36th of the time, or about 30 times in 1100 trials. The number 7, on the other hand, should appear 183 times. The results I obtained are shown here:

```
2 came up 30 times
3 came up 62 times
4 came up 85 times
5 came up 133 times
6 came up 135 times
7 came up 206 times
8 came up 139 times
9 came up 123 times
10 came up 90 times
11 came up 71 times
12 came up 26 times
```

The function of this previous exercise is twofold. First, it shows that (RANDOM :A) + (RANDOM :B) is in no way equivalent to RANDOM (:A + :B). Second, it shows an example of Logo being used to conduct experiments with numbers.

As one last experiment with random numbers, we will explore something called the random walk.

Imagine a drunk at a lamp post who starts walking but who at the end of each step turns by a random amount. What kind of a path will this person trace? The following procedure lets us see a path followed by such a person:

```
TO WALK :steps
REPEAT :steps [FD 5 RT RANDOM 360]
END
```

If we were to enter

```
CS WALK 500
```

we might see the following picture on the screen.

This seemingly frivolous problem is at the heart of several important fields of science, including statistical mechanics. Many models of the physical universe include randomness in them, so random numbers are not only useful in games of chance.

Some of the procedures we have used in this chapter have used such Logo operations as SENTENCE, THING, and BUTFIRST. The next chapter explores two more kinds of data Logo can work with and explains these operations and many more.

V. Computing with Words and Lists

Now that we have explored numbers, it is time to explore computation using the other symbols of our everyday experience. As a language designed for use with symbolic expressions of all types, we expect Logo to be richly endowed with tools for working with words and collections of words. Logo lets us do so much with nonnumeric information that the next two chapters are devoted to this topic.

So far we have used words primarily as the names of variables and as the names of procedures. For example, in the command

MAKE "AGE 21

or in the procedure

TO BOX
REPEAT 4 [FD 20 RT 90]
END

both **AGE** and **BOX** are words. We have also encountered lists, primarily as collections of Logo commands. For example, our definition of **BOX** uses the list

[FD 20 RT 90]

As useful as these applications are, they are just the tip of the computational iceberg. The activities involving lists (and, in similar fashion, words) are called list processing. This aspect of

Logo can be difficult to understand at first, but it is the area from which Logo derives its greatest power.

Before describing Logo's list-processing environment, I want to start with an old Sufi tale whose relevance should become apparent by the end of this chapter.

Duck Soup

A kinsman came to see Nasrudin from the country, and brought a duck. Nasrudin was grateful, had the bird cooked and shared it with his guest.

Presently another visitor arrived. He was a friend, as he said, "of the man who gave you the duck." Nasrudin fed him as well.

This happened several times. Nasrudin's home had become like a restaurant for out-of-town visitors. Everyone was a friend of some removes of the original donor of the duck.

Finally Nasrudin was exasperated. One day there was a knock at the door and a stranger appeared. "I am the friend of the friend of the friend of the man who brought you the duck from the country," he said.

"Come in," said Nasrudin.

They seated themselves at the table, and Nasrudin asked his wife to bring the soup.

When the guest tasted it, it seemed to be nothing more than warm water. "What sort of soup is this?" he asked the Mulla.

"That," said Nasrudin, "is the soup of the soup of the soup of the duck."

(From *The Exploits of the Incomparable Mulla Nasrudin* by Idries Shah, Designist Communications, 1983.)

This Is Predicated to the One I Love

Many of the procedures we will create make use of a set of very useful predicates that Logo provides for us. These predicates can be used to test for the type of data we are looking at (number, word, or list), whether a word or list is empty, whether one word or list is equal to another, whether one word or list is a member of another list, and whether one word is before another in alphabetical order.

Starting with the simplest predicates, **NUMBERP**, **WORDP**, and **LISTP**, it is easy to see how these predicates work.

Enter

```
MAKE "ITEM1 "HOWDY
MAKE "ITEM2 4.56
MAKE "ITEM3 [This is a list of words]
```

If we now test these items by entering

```
PRINT NUMBERP :ITEM1
PRINT NUMBERP :ITEM2
PRINT NUMBERP :ITEM3
```

We will see that only the second query produces a **TRUE** response. Similar experiments with **WORDP** and **LISTP** will produce appropriate responses.

The next set of predicates, **EMPTYP**, **EQUALP**, and **MEMBERP** are the workhorses of Logo. Most of the recursive procedures in this book use at least one of these three predicates. **EMPTYP** simply tests to see if an item (word or list) is empty. If it is, the predicate produces a **TRUE**, otherwise it generates a **FALSE**. The **EQUALP** predicate tests two objects to see if they are equal to each other. This test looks not only at the contents of a word or list, but also at the data type. For example,

```
PRINT EQUALP [Hello] [Hello]
```

will produce **TRUE**, but

```
PRINT EQUALP [Hello] "Hello
```

will produce **FALSE**, because Hello appears as a list in the first object and as a word in the second.

The **MEMBERP** predicate is very handy when you are trying to see if an item is contained in a second object. Its most common use is for testing to see if a particular word is contained in a list. These predicates get heavy use as we progress through this book.

The last predicate I will mention at this time is BEFOREP. This predicate checks to see if one word comes before another word alphabetically. For example,

PRINT BEFOREP "cow "horse

will print TRUE, and

PRINT BEFOREP "cow "axe

will print FALSE. Now, for a Logo peculiarity, see what happens if you enter

PRINT BEFOREP "abracadabra "ZOWIE

This will print FALSE, because Logo treats all uppercase letters as though they come before all lowercase letters (!!?!). If we want to eliminate this case sensitivity, we can fix it with a small procedure:

```
TO ORDEREDP :word1 :word 2
OUTPUT BEFOREP UPPERCASE :word1 UPPERCASE :word2
END
```

This procedure converts word1 and word2 to uppercase before it performs the BEFOREP operation. Logo lets us convert words to uppercase with the UPPERCASE operation and to lowercase with the LOWERCASE operation.

Predicates like BEFOREP are very handy for sorting lists into alphabetical order.

First Things First   A lot of computational activities involving words and lists have the purpose of taking things apart and assembling them. For example, if we examine the word parachute, we can tell that it is made of the letters p, a, r, a, c, h, u, t, and e. Suppose we wanted to create a procedure that separated a word into its individual letters. How would we go about performing this task? As it turns out, we only need to know about two new Logo operations: FIRST and BUTFIRST. To see how these operations work, perform the following experiment.
Enter

PRINT "parachute

(Remember that a literal word must have a quotation mark in front of it, or Logo will treat it as a procedure to be executed.) When this command is entered, we will see the word

parachute

on the display. Next enter:

PRINT FIRST "parachute

This will cause

p

to appear on the display. Finally enter:

PRINT BUTFIRST "parachute

This will cause

arachute

to appear on the display. As you can tell from this exercise, FIRST is an operation that yields the first element of a word, and BUTFIRST (abbreviated BF) yields all but the first element of a word. To extract all the letters from a word one at a time, we can create a recursive procedure that will print the first letter in a word and then the first letter in the letters remaining, and so on until the word is empty:

```
TO BREAKDOWN :item
IF EMPTYP :item [STOP]
PRINT FIRST :item
BREAKDOWN BUTFIRST :item
END
```

This procedure starts by seeing if the item is empty, using the Logo EMPTYP predicate. If there are no more letters in the word, the procedure stops, because there is nothing to do. Otherwise, there is at least one letter to print, and thus the first letter in the item is printed. Next, a copy of BREAKDOWN is used with all but the first letter in the original item. This process repeats itself until the item is empty. To see how it works, enter:

```
BREAKDOWN "parachute
```

This will produce the following display:

```
p
a
r
a
c
h
u
t
e
```

Fresh from our success with words, we can try this same procedure using a list as the item to be broken into its parts. For example, enter:

BREAKDOWN [If you can read this vertically you must like
    poetry]

This will produce:

If
you
can
read
this
vertically
you
must
like
poetry

Instead of breaking the list into a vertical column of letters, the procedure broke the list into a vertical column of words. This is one example of a most beautiful hierarchy that is practiced within Logo: Logo lists, like normal sentences, are comprised of words, and Logo words, as in the words we use every day, are comprised of letters. The FIRST operation will produce a letter if the item it is using is a word, and it will produce a word if the item is a list. In fact, because lists can be made of lists, it is possible for the FIRST of a list to produce another list. For example, if we enter

MAKE "LIST [This [is a list] made [with words] and lists]

and then enter

BREAKDOWN :LIST

we will get the following display. (Note that we want to break down the *thing* associated with the word LIST, not the word itself.)

This
is a list
made
with words
and
lists

By remembering the hierarchy we mentioned above, it is possible to pick any item we want from a list. For example, if we enter

PRINT FIRST BUTFIRST [THIS IS A TEST]

we will see the word IS on the screen because the FIRST item in the BUTFIRST of a list is the second item in the original list. Try to figure out what we will get if we enter

PRINT FIRST FIRST [THIS IS A TEST]

If you try it, you will see the letter T on the screen, because the first item in the list is the word THIS, and therefore the first item in the word is going to be the letter T. To see another example of the hierarchy in action, enter

PRINT FIRST FIRST [[THIS IS] A TEST]

(Notice that this is a list containing another list as well as some words.) This entry will produce the word THIS because the first item in the list is another list ([THIS IS]), and the first item in this list is the word THIS. Now try to figure out what will happen if we enter

PRINT FIRST FIRST FIRST [[THIS IS] A TEST]

You should be able to deduce that this will produce the letter T. Reminds you of duck soup, doesn't it?

Although FIRST and BUTFIRST are adequate for taking lists apart, there are times when it is easier to start from the back of a list or word rather than from the front. Accordingly, Logo has two other list operations to assist you: LAST BUTLAST (abbreviated BL). These commands work just like FIRST and BUTFIRST, but they start at the end rather than at the beginning. For example,

PRINT LAST [THIS A GREAT BOOK SO FAR]

will print

FAR

on the screen, and

PR BUTLAST [THIS IS A GREAT BOOK SO FAR]

will print

THIS IS A GREAT BOOK SO

To test your use of these Logo primitives, figure out what will be printed when we enter:

PRINT FIRST BUTLAST LAST BUTFIRST [TELL ME WHAT YOU
    SEE]

To find the result, start with the operation closest to the list, BUTFIRST. This will produce the list [ME WHAT YOU SEE]. The LAST of this list is the word SEE, the BUTLAST of this word is the word SE, and the first of this word is S, the final result!

Combinations of FIRST and BUTFIRST (or LAST and BUTLAST) can be used to extract any part of a word or list. But, let's face it, typing FIRST BF BF BF BF all the time can be confusing. To make life easier, Logo has a special operation called ITEM that lets you pick any item you want from a word or list. For example,

PRINT ITEM 4 [FLOWERS THAT BLOOM IN THE SPRING ARE NICE]

will print the fourth word in the list: IN. Similarly,

PRINT ITEM 4 "HELICOPTER

will print the letter I.

We can use ITEM and lists to build a great many interesting procedures. For example, we can build a "buzzword phrase generator."

The computer field is replete with an assortment of catch phrases that show how computer literate we are. Whether we talk about an interactive desk-top environment, an artificial intelligence system, or a wimpish modeling hack, we are showing our talents as a computer whiz. Of course, it is important that our use of these phrases be as devoid of meaning as possible, especially if we are writing them for the benefit of someone who knows less about the field than we do. Rather than stress our creative abilities to generate these phrases, we can have Logo do it for us.

The way we will implement the phrase generator is by combining words chosen randomly from three lists. The lists will be stored as the global variables WL1, WL2, and WL3.

When you enter these lists in your computer, use the procedure editor rather than the normal text screen. The reason for this is that the text-screen window only lets you enter expressions less than four lines long, and the editor does not have this constraint. If you want to edit the names of all the global variables, simply enter

EDNS

(for EDit NaMes), and create the variables using the MAKE command:

MAKE "WL1 [artificial synergetic syntonic casual trivial interactive compact expanded wimpish spectacular]

MAKE "WL2 [intelligence modeling conceptualizing inference iconographic [problem - solving] [discovery - based] [age - appropriate] [user - friendly] [desk - top]]

MAKE "WL3 [software hardware program hack system processor computer environment microworld language]

Notice that some of the entries in WL2 are lists themselves. The reason is that a Logo word cannot contain a hyphen, so when we enter a "word" like user-friendly, we make it into a list of three "words": [user - friendly].

Next, we have to create a procedure that picks an element randomly from a list. It so happens that each of our lists is 10 elements long, but when designing Logo procedures, it is usually a good idea to make them as general as possible. Accordingly, we will define a procedure that picks elements randomly from lists of any length:

```
TO RAND :object
OUTPUT ITEM (1 + RANDOM LENGTH :object) :object
END
```

This Logo operation uses another operation, LENGTH, that outputs the length of the object being examined. For example, if the object was [THIS IS A LIST], then LENGTH would output the number 4. LENGTH is another popular Logo procedure we will make considerable use of. It can be defined recursively as shown here.

```
TO LENGTH :object
IF EMPTYP :object [OUTPUT 0]
OUTPUT 1 + LENGTH BUTFIRST :object
END
```

This procedure operates in the following manner. First it looks to see if the object is empty, in which case it outputs a length of 0. If the length isn't 0, it outputs 1 plus the length of everything but the first element of the object. LENGTH will run as many copies of itself as is necessary until there is nothing left in the successively BUTFIRSTed copies of the object. Finally, the sum of all the ones (added to the final 0) will be sent out of the procedure as the final result of the operation.

For example, if we enter

```
PRINT LENGTH "house
```

5 will appear on the screen. (Note that LENGTH works with words as well as with lists, maintaining the hierarchy of data types discussed earlier in this chapter.) Next, enter:

```
PRINT LENGTH [This is a list of several words]
```

This will cause 7 to be printed on the screen. Finally, enter:

```
PRINT LENGTH [This [is a list] [containing lists]]
```

This will cause **3** to be printed on the screen, because the object has three elements in it: one word and two lists.

Of course, we expect that Logo has already anticipated the need for procedures like LENGTH, and in fact, Logo contains a primitive procedure called COUNT that operates just like LENGTH. Every so often it is a good idea to see how one might implement a procedure that is already in Logo. We will continue to use LENGTH in this chapter, but feel free to use COUNT instead.

Now we can test our random word picker, RAND:

REPEAT 10 [PRINT RAND :WL1]

When I gave this command I got the following result:

expanded
interactive
compact
spectacular
trivial
synergetic
interactive
wimpish
casual
casual

Now we are ready to build our last procedure, JARGON:

TO JARGON
OUTPUT (SENTENCE RAND :WL1 RAND :WL2 RAND :WL3)
END

The SENTENCE command is used to assemble items into a list. I will describe its operation in more detail later. For now, let's try our jargon generator to see how it performs:

REPEAT 15 [PRINT JARGON]

This gave me:

wimpish inference hardware
casual intelligence hack
spectacular intelligence hack
syntonic modeling system
spectacular age-appropriate language
expanded intelligence language
wimpish modeling processor
spectacular conceptualizing software
synergetic conceptualizing system
artificial intelligence language
artificial problem-solving processor
wimpish iconographic hardware
syntonic desk-top software
interactive desk-top environment
trivial conceptualizing computer

There are some potentially nonfrivolous uses of a procedure like JARGON. Let's say we are trying to create a new company name, and we have some words or word parts that have the correct "feel." We might want the word to end with a TRONIC or an ETIC, and we may want it to start with a ZAN or a TEX or a RAN or some other letter combination. Once we have created lists of starting, middle, and ending parts of words, we could use JARGON to create some random coupling of these parts. We would then be able to evaluate the computer's choices to see which, if any, sounded right to us. A program similar to this is used by some of the drug companies to choose names for new medications.

There is one procedure that I find quite useful. If you have ever tried to print a long list (one that is over 96 characters long), you may have noticed that the next line of text gets printed over the first line. Also, when you enter long lines on the computer screen, the lines get broken in the middle of words when the right edge of the screen is reached. The following procedure will print long lists in such a manner that they will not have words broken in the middle. Also, if you are printing your lists on the printer, this procedure will make sure the lines don't get printed on top of each other:

```
TO NICEPRINT :object :columns
IF EMPTYP :object [PRINT [] STOP]
IF ((FIRST CURSOR) + LENGTH (FIRST :object)) > :columns
    [PRINT []]
TYPE SENTENCE (FIRST :object)"
NICEPRINT BUTFIRST :object :columns
END
```

This procedure operates in the following fashion. First, it checks to see if **object** is empty, in which case it prints the empty list to give us a new line on the screen and then stops. If **object** isn't empty, the procedure checks to see if the first item in **object** will fit on the line being printed. This checking is done by looking at the cursor position using **CURSOR**, which is a Logo primitive that returns a list containing two numbers. The first number is the column location of the text cursor, and the second number in the list is the row position of the cursor. For this procedure we are only interested in the column number. If the sum of the cursor column and the length of the word to be printed is greater than the number of columns we specify, the procedure will print a new line and then type the word. Otherwise, there is space on the original line for the word to be typed, and it will be typed there. This process is repeated recursively until the last item in **object** has been printed.

The **TYPE** command is similar to **PRINT**, except that it does not cause Logo to issue a return command to advance to a new line. There is one other small but important detail associated with the line containing the **TYPE** command. At first glance you might guess that this line should read:

TYPE FIRST :object

If we entered this (and you should certainly try it), all our words would run together oneafthertheotherlikethis. When we type a sentence consisting of the word and an "empty" word (the quotation mark by itself), Logo appends a space to each word after it is printed.

To try out our new procedure, use the procedure editor to create the following list:

MAKE "TEXT [As the morning sun rose over the eastern hills, its golden rays crept slowly across Dan's face. Slowly, he turned in his bed, hoping for another hour's sleep. But then the phone rang, and Dan sprung awake at the first ring. Little did he know that when he answered that phone he was to learn something that would change his life forever.]

Next, enter

NICEPRINT :TEXT 20

This will produce the following display on the screen:

As the morning sun
rose over the
eastern hills, its
golden rays crept
slowly across Dan's
face. Slowly, he
turned in his bed,
hoping for another
hour's sleep. But
then the phone rang,
and Dan sprung awake
at the first ring.
Little did he know

that when he
answered that phone
he was to learn
something that would
change his life
forever.

This gives us a narrow column of text. To see another extreme, enter

SETWIDTH 80
NICEPRINT :TEXT 78

This will produce:

As the morning sun rose over the eastern hills, its golden rays
crept slowly across Dan's face. Slowly, he turned in his bed,
hoping for another hour's sleep. But then the phone rang, and Dan
sprung awake at the first ring. Little did he know that when he
answered that phone he was to learn something that would change
his life forever.

Notice that whatever column width we choose, the text is printed so that no words are broken at the end of a line. If you were to build a word processor in Logo (and you might want to do that someday), you will find procedures like **NICEPRINT** to be very handy tools.

The House That Jack Built

Before introducing the Logo commands that assemble words and lists, I want to take a small excursion into the mystic field of recursion. At a Logo conference I attended in 1984, someone asked if there were any literary examples of recursion. In fact there are many of them. One that comes to mind immediately is the Mother Goose poem "The House that Jack Built."

This is the house that Jack built.

This is the malt
That lay in the house
That Jack built.

etc.

Because of the apparent recursive structure of this poem, it seemed like a good idea to try to create a Logo procedure that would type all 12 verses of the poem recursively, starting with a list containing all the lines. The following set of two procedures (along with the global variable LINES) perform this task for us:

```
TO POEM :num
IF EQUALP :num 0 [STOP]
POEM :num − 1
PR [This is]
PRINTLINES :num
END
```

```
TO PRINTLINES :num
IF EQUALP :num 0 [PR [] STOP]
PR ITEM :num :LINES
PRINTLINES :num − 1
END
```

```
MAKE "LINES [[The house that Jack built.] [The malt that lay in]
    [The rat that ate] [The cat that killed] [The dog that worried]
    [The cow with the crumpled horn that tossed] [The maiden
    all forlorn that milked] [The man all tattered and torn that
    kissed] [The priest all shaven and shorn that married] [The
    cock that crowed in the morn that waked] [The farmer
    sowing his corn that kept] [The horse and the hound and the
    horn that belonged to]]
```

We can start by exploring how these procedures work. The procedure POEM starts with a value of num that indicates how many verses of the poem are to be printed. First this procedure makes copies of itself with local values of num ranging from the original value down to 1. Next, the copy of POEM with num equal to 1 prints the line This is and then executes the procedure PRINTLINES with a value of num equal to 1. The PRINTLINES procedure recursively prints the items in the list LINES, starting with the item value equal to num, and working backwards to 1. As each verse is printed, PRINTLINES prints a blank line before returning to the next higher level of POEM. The following text shows the version of this poem as it was printed by entering

POEM 12

This is
The house that Jack built.

This is
The malt that lay in
The house that Jack built.

This is
The rat that ate
The malt that lay in
The house that Jack built.

This is
The cat that killed
The rat that ate
The malt that lay in
The house that Jack built.

This is
The dog that worried
The cat that killed
The rat that ate
The malt that lay in
The house that Jack built.

This is
The cow with the crumpled horn that tossed
The dog that worried
The cat that killed
The rat that ate
The malt that lay in
The house that Jack built.

This is
The maiden all forlorn that milked
The cow with the crumpled horn that tossed
The dog that worried
The cat that killed
The rat that ate
The malt that lay in
The house that Jack built.

This is
The man all tattered and torn that kissed
The maiden all forlorn that milked
The cow with the crumpled horn that tossed
The dog that worried
The cat that killed
The rat that ate
The malt that lay in
The house that Jack built.

This is
The priest all shaven and shorn that married
The man all tattered and torn that kissed
The maiden all forlorn that milked
The cow with the crumpled horn that tossed
The dog that worried
The cat that killed
The rat that ate
The malt that lay in
The house that Jack built.

This is
The cock that crowed in the morn that waked
The priest all shaven and shorn that married
The man all tattered and torn that kissed
The maiden all forlorn that milked
The cow with the crumpled horn that tossed
The dog that worried
The cat that killed
The rat that ate
The malt that lay in
The house that Jack built.

This is
The farmer sowing his corn that kept
The cock that crowed in the morn that waked
The priest all shaven and shorn that married
The man all tattered and torn that kissed
The maiden all forlorn that milked
The cow with the crumpled horn that tossed
The dog that worried
The cat that killed
The rat that ate
The malt that lay in
The house that Jack built.

This is
The horse and the hound and the horn that belonged to
The farmer sowing his corn that kept
The cock that crowed in the morn that waked
The priest all shaven and shorn that married
The man all tattered and torn that kissed
The maiden all forlorn that milked
The cow with the crumpled horn that tossed
The dog that worried
The cat that killed
The rat that ate
The malt that lay in
The house that Jack built.

You can create some of your own versions of this poem by making a new version of **LINES**. For example:

This is
The program that Jill wrote.

This is
The bug that lay in
The program that Jill wrote.

This is
The patch that fixed
The bug that lay in
The program that Jill wrote.

Now that we know how to extract information from lists, it is time to learn how to assemble lists from separate parts.

Putting Things Together

Logo has several primitives designed to let us assemble words and lists from separate parts. If the previous commands we have explored can be thought of as the scissors that cut things apart, the primitives described next make up the glue that puts things together.

We have already encountered one of these primitives, **SENTENCE**. The function of this operation is to take two or more words or lists and combine them into a single list.

To explore the function of these operations, we will make use of the Logo **SHOW** primitive. **SHOW** is similar to **PRINT**, except that it leaves the outer brackets in place when printing lists.

To explore **SENTENCE**, enter

SHOW SENTENCE [This is a combination] [of two lists.]

This will print

[This is a combination of two lists.]

Logo expects SENTENCE (or its short form, SE) to have only two arguments. If we want to make a list with other than two arguments, we must enclose the entire expression in parentheses. For example,

SHOW (SENTENCE [We can use a list, a] "word [and another list.])

produces:

[We can use a list, a word and another list.]

As we have already seen, SENTENCE is a heavily used Logo primitive. But what if we want to combine two lists into a new list but we want each list to retain its own "listness" identity? For this activity we can use the LIST primitive: For example,

SHOW LIST [Here is one list] [and here is another.]

will produce

[[Here is one list] [and here is another]]

The SENTENCE operation "flattens" two lists into one, and the LIST command creates a new list containing, as elements, the two argument lists. As with SENTENCE, LIST can take more than two arguments if the entire expression is enclosed in parentheses.

There are cases in which LIST and SENTENCE can produce the same result. For example,

SHOW LIST "Hi "there

and

SHOW SENTENCE "Hi "there

both produce

[Hi there]

If we want to convert a single word into a list, we can use either SENTENCE or LIST. For example,

SHOW (SENTENCE "Hello)
SHOW (LIST "Hello)

We can also use a special Logo primitive

SHOW PARSE "Hello

All three of these examples will produce

[Hello]

on the screen.

Although you will probably find more uses for constructing lists than for constructing words, it is important to have a tool for building a word. The Logo primitive that performs this task is, not surprisingly, WORD. If we enter

SHOW WORD "real "ly

we will see

really

on the screen. This is a handy type of operation to use in programs; for example, when we want to create a dialog program
in which the computer responds with a word in tense other
than the one we used. To illustrate this, enter the following
procedure:


```
TO CONVERSE
LOCAL "response
MAKE "response LAST READLIST
MAKE "response WORD :response "ed
PRINT (SENTENCE [Have you] :response [before?])
CONVERSE
END
```


This procedure uses a variable, **response**, that we have
made "local" to this procedure with the LOCAL command.
CONVERSE will wait for us to enter a line of text and press
the return key (using the READLIST operation) and then
append the letters **ed** to the end of the last word in our response. Finally, a new sentence is printed on the screen using
this new word we have created. Each time we enter a line of
text using CONVERSE, the computer will print its response:

I like to walk
Have you walked before?

I like to climb
Have you climbed before?

I like to fish
Have you fished before?

Before you get too impressed with this "natural language" program, enter

I like to fly
Have you flyed before?

We obviously have a long way to go before we can use a true past-tense generator, but it's easy to see why WORD will be a useful component of such a procedure.

So far, our operations have made lists and words out of whole cloth. There are times when you will want to append items to already-existing lists. Logo's primitives LPUT and FPUT are designed for just such occasions. The only difference between these two operations is that LPUT appends an item to the end of a list (Last PUT), and FPUT places the item at the front of a list (First PUT). For example,

SHOW LPUT "test [This is a]

will produce

[This is a test]

and

SHOW FPUT "Test [This is a]

will produce

[test This is a]

Both **FPUT** and **LPUT** operate by placing the first argument inside the list that comprises the second argument. The first argument can be a word or a list, and the second argument must be a list. So if we enter

SHOW LPUT [This is a] [test]

we will get

[test [this is a]]

LPUT and FPUT can (and are) used to construct very elaborate list structures. Because lists of various types can be used to create new computational objects as we shall see later, LPUT and FPUT will be getting a lot of use as we progress through this book.

To show just how useful list processing can be, the next chapter explores several list-processing projects that touch ever so gently on the fringes of artificial intelligence.

VI.

More on Words and Lists

In this chapter we explore applications of list processing and expand our library of Logo tools. In order to do this we need a context, a domain in which to create Logo procedures. The number of programming areas to which Logo can be applied is quite large—word processing, video games, and accounting systems, to name just three. But, unlike some other programming languages, Logo can also be used to explore topics in the field of artificial intelligence; and that is the topic I have chosen to explore in this chapter.

Artificial Intelligence

The domain of artificial-intelligence research is one that has very few neutral participants or observers. The more vociferous and flamboyant researchers have been known for their belief that the human intellect is capable of computer modeling and that we are thus nothing more than sophisticated computers ourselves. The more vociferous and flamboyant detractors claim that any research into artificial intelligence demeans the human spirit and should not be pursued.

I have a more moderate view: that the goal of artificial intelligence is nothing more than to make computers do things that would require intelligence if they were done by people. Note that I am making no claims that the computer is "thinking" nor that the computer's intelligence is of the same nature or form as our own. When used in this context, references to artificial intelligence are similar to references to artificial flight (the domain of airplanes). Artificial flight is the result of making machines do things that would require flight if they were done by birds. The similarities between airplanes and birds are tenuous at best (consider seating capacity, for example), and yet we were encouraged in our design of such machines by our studies of birds and other flying animals.

The byproducts of artificial intelligence range from programs that help oil companies decide where to drill to reading machines for the blind to the well-known work on developing chess games that improve with practice.

A more compelling reason I have chosen this topic is that computer languages such as Logo, LISP, and PROLOG were designed to satisfy the needs of programmers in this field of endeavor. Consequently, one can write programs in Logo that do things that are virtually impossible to do in other languages. If you come to Logo from a language such as BASIC, some of what you see in this chapter will carry you far beyond the capabilities of your former language.

One of our projects will create a Logo program that lets the turtle solve a maze. Most would agree that it takes intelligence for a human to solve a maze, so we might be justified in thinking of our maze-solving program as an example of artificial intelligence. To make our task more challenging we will add a feature to our program that is similar to "intelligent" human problem solving: after the turtle solves the maze the first time, it will "remember" the solution so it can solve it very quickly the next time it encounters the same maze. The first solution will take place by trial and error, and then the turtle will write a procedure to solve the maze correctly—with no false turns.

The ability of Logo procedures to create other procedures distinguishes it from many other computer languages. Because of this unique aspect of Logo-like languages, it is important that we preface our maze solver with an introduction to the way Logo transforms data into procedures.

From Data to Procedures

We will begin by taking a close look at a Logo primitive you have used so many times that you may not have ever stopped to grasp the full implications of its actions. The primitive I have in mind is REPEAT.

From your experience with turtle graphics you already know that REPEAT is a command that accepts two arguments. The first argument is a number and the second is a list of commands to be carried out the prescribed number of times. Normally we create the list explicitly when we write our symbolic expression:

REPEAT 5 [FD 100 RT 144]

When this command is executed it draws a five-point star on the screen. It is important to realize that the list in this expression is a collection of four words: FD, 100, RT, and 144. The fact that these words combine to form two Logo commands (FD 100 and RT 144) is important to the correct operation of REPEAT, but otherwise there is nothing special about this list. For example, one could create the following list:

MAKE "OPERATION [PRINT [Hi there, everyone]]

This list is comprised of a word (PRINT) and a list ([Hi there, everyone]). If we were to print the list by entering

PRINT :OPERATION

we would see

PRINT [Hi there, everyone]

on the screen. On the other hand, we can give the command:

REPEAT 5 :OPERATION

which will instead produce:

Hi there, everyone
Hi there, everyone
Hi there, everyone
Hi there, everyone
Hi there, everyone

It is obvious from these examples that PRINT and REPEAT treat the list OPERATION quite differently. The PRINT command simply prints the contents of the list, and REPEAT interprets it as a Logo statement to be executed. This dual role of Logo words and lists—as data and as program commands—gives it the capability to be used as a tool for the automatic generation of new procedures.

Logo facilitates this automatic generation in two ways. The first is through the direct execution of lists (using REPEAT, for example), and the second is through the transformation of the list into a bona fide Logo procedure through the use of the DEFINE primitive (described at the end of this section).

Many applications need to be able to execute a list of Logo expressions. If the list is to be executed more than once, REPEAT is the appropriate command; but quite often the list is executed only once. Rather than use, for example,

REPEAT 1 :OPERATION

we can use the Logo primitive RUN:

RUN :OPERATION

In terms of its operational consequences, RUN is similar to REPEAT 1. To illustrate a good use for RUN, consider the case in which a procedure is executed several times with different arguments. We might start with this procedure:

```
TO LETTER :name
NICEPRINT (SENTENCE [Please note that your child,] :name [, is
    making excellent progress in our programming class.]) 38
PRINT []
END
```

(Note that this procedure uses NICEPRINT from the previous chapter.) If we want to create a lot of these notes to send home, we might enter

```
LETTER [Jacques Absorber]
LETTER [Phil E. Buster]
LETTER [Mary deRich]
```

Alternatively, we could place all the names in a list and map each of them to LETTER in turn using a command like:

```
MAP "LETTER [[Jacques Absorber] [Phil E. Buster] [Mary deRich]]
```

One implementation of MAP can be written this way:

```
TO MAP :command :argumentlist
IF EMPTYP :argumentlist [STOP]
RUN LIST :command FIRST :argumentlist
MAP :command BUTFIRST :argumentlist
END
```

When this implementation is used with the example shown above, it produces the following result:

```
Please note that your child, Jacques
Absorber , is making excellent
progress in our programming class.
```

Please note that your child, Phil E.
Buster , is making excellent progress
in our programming class.

Please note that your child, Mary
deRich , is making excellent progress
in our programming class.

The function of the RUN command in MAP is to execute the
Logo expression that was assembled from the list put together
by the procedure itself.

Although RUN (and REPEAT) have the effect of executing
symbolic expressions in the form of lists, these expressions are
not transformed into bona fide Logo procedures. If we are to
grant Logo status as a first-class programming language, we
should expect it to have the capacity to define Logo procedures
that are in all ways indistinguishable from those you might enter from the keyboard.

This task is carried out through the use of the DEFINE
primitive. DEFINE takes two arguments. The first is the name
of the procedure to be defined, and the second is a list of arguments and expressions that are to become the definition of the
procedure. For example, if we were to enter

DEFINE "SQUARE [[size] [REPEAT 4 [FD :size RT 90]]]

this would result in the creation of the following procedure:

```
TO SQUARE :size
REPEAT 4 [FD :size RT 90]
END
```

The first element in the definition list *must* be a list of arguments for the defined procedure. Note that we need not include the colon (:) in front of variable names in this list. If the

procedure has no arguments, we must begin the definition
with the empty list. For example:

DEFINE "CIRCLE [[] [REPEAT 360 [FD 1 RT 1]]]

DEFINE has the task of converting a list of data into a Logo
procedure. Because we may want to have a Logo procedure
modify another, existing Logo procedure, it is handy to have a
way of converting a Logo procedure back to a data list. This
can be done with the **TEXT** operation. For example, if we enter

PRINT TEXT "SQUARE

we will see:

[size] [REPEAT 4 [FD :size RT 90]]

As a practical application for **TEXT**, we will construct a
procedure that displays procedure listings in the same form as
they appear in this book: expressions that are longer than one
line are indented a few spaces to make them easier to read. An
additional feature of this procedure is evident when you list
your procedures on the printer. Very long procedure lines wrap
over themselves on the printer, making them illegible. Using
our new procedure to list procedures to the printer, this problem disappears. Procedures of the type described in this section
are called "pretty printers." True pretty printing would look at
the form of the procedure and produce indentation that was
symbolic of the nesting and branching that takes place in the
procedure. Although you are free to explore that aspect of pretty
printing, we will keep our procedures much simpler here.

From the top level we want to be able to invoke the pretty-
print routine by entering **PPRINT** followed by the procedure
name and the number of columns in which the procedure is to

be listed. The PPRINT procedure has the task of converting the procedure to a list, printing the word TO followed by the procedure name and the arguments it uses, and then printing out the rest of the procedure in a form that looks nice on the screen. This is accomplished with the main procedure:

```
TO PPRINT :procedure :columns
PRINT []
LOCAL "contents
MAKE "contents TEXT :procedure
PRINT (SENTENCE "TO :procedure FIRST :contents)
EXTRACT BUTFIRST :contents :columns
END
```

This procedure uses the TEXT primitive to convert the named procedure to a list. Next, we need to explore the function of EXTRACT. This procedure has two jobs. The first is to print each line of the Logo procedure so that it fits within the column boundaries. If one line is longer than the column boundaries it must be split up into two or more lines in which the extra lines are indented from the first by a certain amount (say three spaces). Second, when all the lines have been printed, EXTRACT prints the Logo END command at the end of the procedure:

```
TO EXTRACT :item :columns
IF EMPTYP :item [PRINT "END STOP]
NICEPRINT FIRST :item :columns 3
EXTRACT BUTFIRST :item :columns
END
```

EXTRACT makes heavy use of NICEPRINT. In order to make NICEPRINT work properly we have to make two modifications to it. First we need to add an indentation parameter that will cause any lines after the first to appear indented from the first line. Then we need to have embedded lists

appear with their brackets intact. Accordingly, we must use the
LIST rather than the SENTENCE primitive when writing this
procedure. To make this new version of NICEPRINT we must
modify our old copy to look like this:

```
TO NICEPRINT :object :columns :indent
IF EMPTYP :object [PRINT [] STOP]
IF ((FIRST CURSOR) + COUNT (FIRST :object)) > :columns [PRINT
    [] REPEAT :indent [TYPE CHAR 32]]
TYPE LIST (FIRST :object) "
NICEPRINT BUTFIRST :object :columns :indent
END
```

To see how this all works, let's use PPRINT to list itself.
First, for reference, let's see what the normal procedure printer
(PO) does. If we are using the 40-column text mode on our
computer and enter

```
PO "PPRINT
```

we will get the following on the screen:

```
TO PPRINT :procedure :columns
PRINT []
LOCAL "contents
MAKE "contents TEXT :procedure
PRINT ( SENTENCE "TO :procedure FIRST :!
    contents )
EXTRACT BUTFIRST :contents :columns
END
```

Notice the exclamation point to indicate when a line is longer
than 40 columns. Next, enter

```
PPRINT "PPRINT 38
```

This will produce the following display:

```
TO PPRINT procedure columns
PRINT []
LOCAL "contents
MAKE "CONTENTS TEXT :procedure
PRINT ( SENTENCE "TO
      :procedure FIRST
      :contents )
EXTRACT BUTFIRST :contents :columns
END
```

This listing has no words split in the middle, and there is one long line that is shown in the indented form. Notice that the dots are missing from the arguments in the first line. We can modify PPRINT to put them in place. To make a really compressed listing, enter

```
PPRINT "PPRINT 20
```

This will produce a very narrow listing:

```
TO PPRINT procedure columns
PRINT []
LOCAL "contents
MAKE "contents TEXT
      :procedure
PRINT ( SENTENCE "TO
      :procedure FIRST
      :contents )
EXTRACT BUTFIRST
      :contents
      :columns
END
```

As you continue to use PPRINT you will find procedures for which it fails to work properly. This failure occurs when printing a line that contains a long embedded list. The

EXTRACT procedure could be modified to look at each line recursively so it peers into the structure of any embedded lists in the line. This would solve the problem but would take us far beyond the scope of this exercise—which was to show an example of the utility of TEXT. You should now know enough about Logo to create a pretty-print routine that will work properly for all legitimate Logo procedures. Rather than pursue that topic, let's move on to our main exercise: the construction of a maze-solving system.

Solving Mazes

Our goal is to construct a set of Logo procedures that solve a maze and generate a new Logo procedure containing the solution of the maze. There are many types of mazes we might consider; they can be as simple as a single path with no dead ends or as complex as a maze with numerous solutions. To keep our illustration as brief and understandable as possible, we will build a maze solver that works with the simplest of mazes. Once you understand this environment you can build more elaborate maze solvers on your own.

As a starting point we must have a maze to solve. The streets of our maze should be easy to see, so I have chosen to build them from rectangles eight units wide. The following procedure lets us build a street of any length:

```
TO RECT :len
LT 90 FD 4 RT 90
FD :len RT 90 FD 8 RT 90
FD :len RT 90 FD 4 RT 90
FD (:len − 4) FILL
END
```

The FILL command in this procedure is a powerful Logo primitive that fills any shape up to a boundary of the same color as the FILL color. For our maze we will keep the pen at the default (white) color, although you should feel free to change this.

Two other characteristics of **RECT** are worth mentioning. First, the street width is centered around the turtle; second, the turtle finishes near the end of the street it has just drawn. This positions the turtle at the proper location to start drawing the next street. For example, enter

CS RECT 50

This command draws a filled vertical rectangle with the turtle moved to the end of the street.

We will build our maze so it has only 90-degree turns; this is an arbitrary choice. By keeping the magnitude of the turns fixed we simplify the maze solver's task. We do of course allow turns to the left or right so our maze solver has *some* work to do.

To continue to build our maze we might enter the following commands:

```
LT 90 RECT 40
RT 90 RECT 20
RT 90 RECT 60
```

As a starting maze for our examination, let's use this one:

```
TO MAZE
CS PD HT
RECT 40 LT 90 RECT 30 RT 90
RECT 20 RT 90 RECT 50 RT 90
RECT 50 LT 90 RECT 20 LT 90
RECT 70 LT 90 RECT 100 LT 90
RECT 100 LT 90 RECT 120 LT 90
RECT 40 RT 90 RECT 50
PU HOME ST
END
```

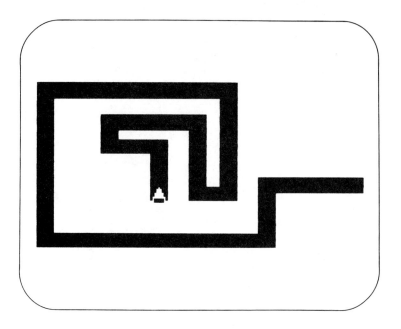

Notice that the **MAZE** procedure places the turtle at the home position when it is finished. One property of the maze we created is that it ends with an *X*-coordinate on the screen in excess of 100. We can test for the *X*-portion of the turtle position to see if the maze is finished. As with the other parameters we have chosen, feel free to pick new conditions for the end of the maze if you wish.

The next topic we need to explore is how we can tell whether the turtle is on the street. The Logo predicate **DOTP** "looks" to see if there is a dot at a specified position on the screen. If there is, it returns **TRUE**; otherwise it returns **FALSE**. The position of interest to us is the turtle's location, given by the primitive operation **POS**.

For example, if we enter

PRINT DOTP POS

the screen will show **TRUE** because the turtle is resting over the start of the maze. If we now enter

BK 10 PRINT DOTP POS

the screen will show **FALSE** because we have moved the turtle off the maze. When using **DOTP**, remember to move the turtle with its pen up, or else it will always give the **TRUE** response.

Now that we know how to tell if the turtle is on the screen, we can create a procedure that lets us know when the turtle gets to the end of the road. For example:

```
TO CRAWL :dist
IF NOT DOTP POS [OUTPUT :dist]
FD 1
OUTPUT CRAWL :dist + 1
END
```

This procedure serves two distinct functions at once. First, it moves the turtle incrementally along a street until it gets to the end. Second, it is an operation that produces a result equal to the distance traveled by the turtle. To see how this works, enter

```
CS PD
RECT 60 PU HOME
PRINT SENTENCE [The turtle went forward] CRAWL 0
```

This moves the turtle to the end of the street and prints on the screen:

The turtle went forward 61

We now have two key elements for our maze solver: we have a way of moving the turtle forward by trial and error until it gets to the end of the street and we have a measure of how far the turtle moved. This is useful for building our "solved maze" procedure.

Once we have reached the end of the street we should move back a few units to place the turtle back on the maze. We are then ready to have the turtle find a new direction in which to move. This can be accomplished with another hybrid procedure:

```
TO NEWHEADING
LT 90 FD 7
IF DOTP POS [BK 7 OUTPUT [LT 90]]
BK 7 RT 180 FD 7
IF DOTP POS [BK 7 OUTPUT [RT 90]]
BK 7 RT 90
OUTPUT [RT 180]
END
```

This procedure uses trial and error to find the direction of the next street. First it turns the turtle to the left and moves forward seven units to see if there is a new street in this direction. If there is, it moves the turtle back but leaves it in this heading and outputs the list [LT 90] to indicate the new direction the turtle has turned. If there is no street to the left, it checks to see if there is one to the right. If there is none to the right, the turtle is at a dead end, so it turns around to go back the way it came.

Because **NEWHEADING** is an operation, it can be incorporated into a modified **CRAWL** procedure to generate the set of movement and turning data we need to solve our maze. We will call the new version of CRAWL **MOVEIT:**

```
TO MOVEIT :dist
IF NOT DOTP POS [BK4 OUTPUT (SENTENCE [FD] :dist − 4
    NEWHEADING)]
FD 1
OUTPUT MOVEIT :dist + 1
END
```

Testing this procedure is fairly easy. First we should create a street or two for the turtle to negotiate:

```
CS PD
RECT 60 RT 90 RECT 60
PU HOME
```

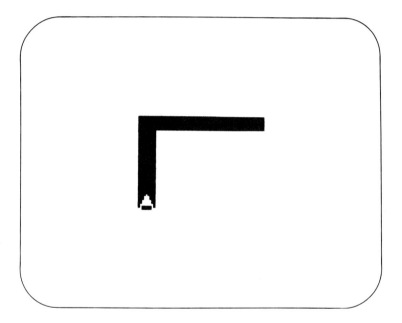

Next, enter

```
PRINT MOVEIT 0
```

This causes the turtle to crawl along the first street until it reaches the end. Then it searches for the next branch. Once it finds the branch to the right it prints

```
FD 57 RT 90
```

and stops. Notice that the printed commands correspond to the solution of the first leg of the maze.

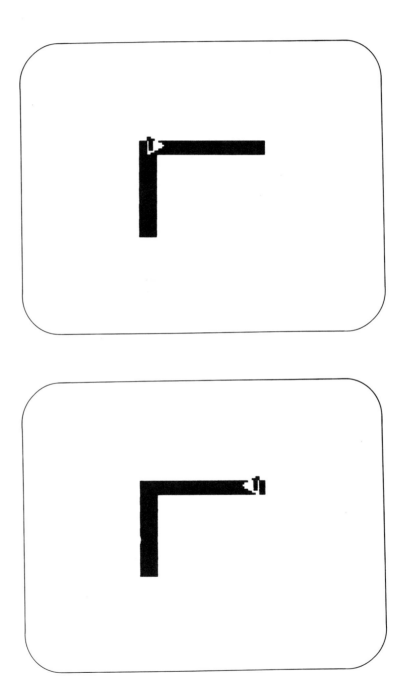

The solution of a complete maze takes place by the repeated application of MOVEIT. But we must also decide what we are going to do with the lists of commands that are being generated each time MOVEIT is used. We need to append the output of MOVEIT to a list containing the history of the turtle's motions. This history list will then be used to define our new procedure.

Our maze-solver routine looks like this:

```
TO SOLVEIT
IF (FIRST POS) > 100 [STOP]
MAKE "HIST LPUT MOVEIT 0 :HIST
SOLVEIT
END
```

Because we can't append anything to a nonexistent list, we must initialize HIST. We can accomplish this task and draw our maze with the following procedure:

```
TO SETUP
MAKE "HIST [[]]
MAZE
END
```

This procedure starts HIST off as a list containing an empty list. The reason for the embedded empty list is that the procedure we will create has no parameters, and the first element of a list used with the DEFINE command must contain the parameter list. Because each appended entry will follow the initial empty list, HIST will have the form expected by the DEFINE command.

The solution of our maze is given by:

```
TO SOLUTION
SOLVEIT
DEFINE "FASTSOLUTION :HIST
END
```

If we now enter

SETUP
SOLUTION

we will see the turtle solve the maze by trial and error. This time-consuming solution will result in the turtle reaching the end in about 60 seconds.

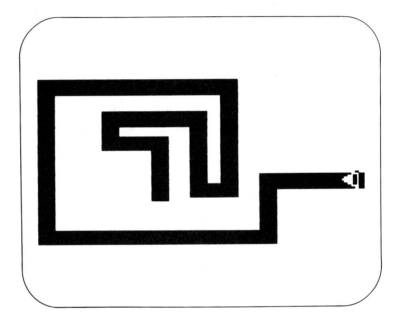

If we now enter

HOME
FASTSOLUTION

we will see the turtle solve the maze almost immediately. To see the solution written by our maze-solving program, enter

PO "FASTSOLUTION

This will produce the following listing:

```
TO FASTSOLUTION
FD 37 LT 90
FD 27 RT 90
FD 16 RT 90
FD 49 RT 90
FD 48 LT 90
FD 16 LT 90
FD 68 LT 90
FD 99 LT 90
FD 98 LT 90
FD 119 LT 90
FD 38 RT 90
FD 46 RT 180
END
```

This procedure was written entirely by the computer!

Create some more mazes of your own and notice that each new version of **FASTSOLUTION** will be created specifically to solve your new maze.

This small example of artificial-intelligence programming made no use of human interaction. Our next example is at the opposite extreme: it depends critically on human interaction with the system.

Twenty Questions

As an example of artificial intelligence, imagine a program designed to play the game Twenty Questions. In this game the computer has "thought" of something whose identity you are to guess by asking questions that can be answered with a yes or no. A typical dialog from the program described in this section is shown below. The computer's response is almost always limited to **yes** or **no**:

I have thought of something whose identity you are to guess. Please ask questions that can be answered with a yes or no answer.

Is it a thing?
No.

Is it a place?
Yes.

Is this place in the United States?
No.

How about Europe.

You didn't ask a question. Please end your response with a question mark.

Is it in Europe?
Yes.

Is it in England?
No.

Is it in France?
Yes.

Is it a building?
No.

Is it a river?
No.

Is it a city?
Yes.

Is it Paris?
No.

Is it LeHavre?
Yes.

You might think this game is behaving quite intelligently. It appears to handle unrestricted English text quite well, and it seems to know a great deal about the context associated with the correct answer. Of course, as the program is run, there are certain delays that one expects with any large program—especially one that has the apparent capabilities of this one. In fact, the game program I just described does not play Twenty Questions at all. It cheats. But it is the method by which it cheats and the reasons the game appears to work so well that make it a good subject for exploration in this chapter.

If you look at the questions entered by the user and the responses from the computer, you might be able to discern a pattern. Notice that the program looks for the existence of a question mark, which has nothing to do with the game except that it pins down the location of the last word in the question. If you look at the last letter in each question and correlate it to the response, you will see that questions ending in consonants generate a no answer and those ending in vowels generate a yes.

The reason this works at all for this game is that most of us who have played Twenty Questions know that we have only a limited number of queries from which we are to find the answer to the puzzle; therefore, we tend to go from the general to the specific. If we asked if the item was a person and we were told no, we would not be likely to then ask if it was our good friend Marsha (for which it would respond with a yes). By generating nonrandom responses based on the occurrence of certain letters, this version of the game not only lets us play Twenty Questions *by* ourselves, but it also lets us play it *with* ourselves. If you are normally very good at this game you will be good at the computer version as well. The easiest way to find out that the game is "cheating" is to let it be used by someone who is not at all good at playing the real game.

In case you want to study people's response with this game yourself, the procedures for it are shown below:

```
TO TWENTY
NICEPRINT [I have thought of something whose identity you are to
    guess. Please ask questions that can be answered with a yes
    or no answer.] 38 0
REPEAT 20 [PRINT [] QUESTION PRINT []]
PRINT [You did very well!]
END


TO QUESTION
LOCAL "response
MAKE "response GOODWORD
WAIT RANDOM 200
IF MEMBERP UPPERCASE LAST BUTLAST :response
    [A E I O U Y] [PRINT "Yes.] [PRINT "No.]
END


TO GOODWORD
LOCAL "response
MAKE "response LAST READLIST
IF EQUALP LAST :response "? [OUTPUT :response]
NICEPRINT [You didn't ask a question. Please end your response
    with a question mark.] 38 0
PRINT []
OUTPUT GOODWORD
END
```

The operation of this program is quite simple—not at all what one might expect as a result of playing the game. The main procedure, **TWENTY**, prints the opening message on the screen and then uses the **QUESTION** procedure 20 times. (The **PRINT** commands give some space between the questions.) After all 20 questions have been answered, **TWENTY** prints a closing message and stops.

The **QUESTION** procedure uses the operation **GOOD-WORD** to extract the last word of a user's question. The program then halts for a random time of up to a little over two seconds through the use of the **WAIT** command. This delay is important because it helps convince the user that the computer is actually "thinking" about its response to the question. You may want to adjust the waiting time in your own experiments with this program to see what results you get. The next-to-last character (**LAST BUTLAST**) in the word stored in response is then examined to see if it is a vowel. The **UPPERCASE** command capitalizes this letter, because the list of vowels is composed entirely of uppercase letters. If this letter is a vowel, the computer prints **yes**; otherwise it prints **no**.

The **GOODWORD** procedure accepts a line of text from the keyboard and checks to see if the last character in the line is a question mark. If it is, the last word (including the question mark) is passed out of the procedure. Otherwise, the user is given a message and **GOODWORD** is used again until the user makes the proper type of response.

Here is another sample dialog with this game:

I have thought of something whose
identity you are to guess. Please ask
questions that can be answered with a
yes or no answer.

Oh good. I'm ready to play the game — are you?
Yes.

Wait a minute - have I used a question already?
Yes.

Boy - I'd better get going. Is it vegetable?
Yes.

Good! Hmmm - is it something you would put on a pizza?
Yes.

How about onions?
No.

Perhaps some peppers?
No.

But is it a spice?
Yes.

Is it oregano?
Yes.

Terrific! - But did you really understand my questions?
No.

I have been asked if this program is an example of artificial intelligence. My response is that it emphasizes the "artificial" aspect of artificial intelligence. The most important thing that can be said of this game is that it gives the same responses that would be given by a "real" program that was directing the player to the same answer. The fact that the guidance given by the present program is not based on the full text of the user's question is a detail; the program uses feature extraction as a basis for generating its response. Feature extraction plays an important role in much of the "serious" work in artificial intelligence. When writing a program to recognize hand-printed characters, for example, it is too time consuming to have the computer monitor and analyze every nuance in a printed character. Instead, the system is written in such a way that it looks for certain features that are indicative of certain characters.

In this sense, our version of Twenty Questions has something in common with other, more intelligent programs. In fact, one of the famous definitions of intelligent behavior in machines is the so-called Turing Test, named after Alan Turing. In this test, a user is placed in a closed room containing two computer terminals. One of the terminals is connected to a computer and the other to another terminal staffed by a human being. By typing questions at each terminal and judging the responses, the user is asked to determine which terminal is connected to a computer and which is staffed by a human. If the user cannot tell which is which, the Turing Test concludes that the computer was behaving intelligently.

Our own Twenty Questions program is a second-order Turing Test—it behaves in a similar fashion to a program that would actually play a game of Twenty Questions, assuming it had a sufficiently large knowledge base and could handle natural language queries. Of course, a "real" Twenty Questions program would be a massive undertaking, but from the user's perspective it wouldn't respond in a way different from the little one we created. Because the user's perceptions are important here, it is an open question as to whether our program is behaving intelligently.

Eliza and the Doctor

Having shown one example of an artificial intelligence program that cheats, I would be remiss if I didn't devote some space to discussing the most famous (and one of the least intelligent) of the artificial-intelligence programs ever written. This program, ELIZA, was written by Joseph Weizenbaum in 1964 to simulate the role of a Rogerian psychotherapist engaged in an initial interview with a patient. This environment was easy for him to imitate because much of the therapeutic technique consists of drawing the patient out by reflecting his or her statements. It is important, in any computer simulation, to limit the scope of the user dialog; otherwise, one can encounter so much varied material that the analysis program would grow tremendously in size. For example, one of the first clues to indicate that **TWENTY** cheats is that it has no restrictions on subject matter. If we were to create an expert system that played a serious game of Twenty Questions, it would need access to entire libraries of information. This limitation of scope has other consequences (as we shall see for ELIZA). It makes these programs work well within a limited domain but causes them to fail precipitously as the boundaries of this domain are reached. This is very different from the behavior of a human expert. Each of us may know a great deal about a specific limited topic, but we all contain a wealth of general information to which we have access outside this limited domain.

A typical dialog fragment from Weizenbaum's program is shown below. The machine response is in uppercase letters.

Men are all alike.
IN WHAT WAY?
They're always bugging us about something or other.
CAN YOU THINK OF A SPECIFIC EXAMPLE
Well, my boyfriend made me come here.
YOUR BOYFRIEND MADE YOU COME HERE
He says I'm depressed much of the time.
I AM SORRY TO HEAR YOU ARE DEPRESSED
It's true. I am unhappy.
DO YOU THINK COMING HERE WILL HELP YOU NOT TO BE
    UNHAPPY
I need some help, that much seems certain.
WHAT WOULD IT MEAN IF YOU GOT SOME HELP

(From *Computer Power and Human Reasoning* by J. Weizenbaum, W.H. Freeman & Company, 1976. pp 3–4.)

If you had never seen TWENTY you might be very impressed with this dialog. But knowing what you now know about list processing, you could probably figure out what ELIZA is doing. It isn't "understanding" the user's text any more than TWENTY did. It is, however, several steps above TWENTY in its feature extraction capabilities. Before exploring some of the philosophical implications of ELIZA, we should explore how we might create a small version of it ourselves. The program we will create, DOCTOR, has two major activities: it analyzes the user's statement and responds appropriately. The response can have any of several forms, depending on the user's statement. For example, if the user enters

I am depressed.

the computer might respond with

Tell me why you are depressed.

This response is generated by replacing I am with you are and adding the prefix phrase Tell me why. One can use any of several prefix phrases, chosen at random. For example: I understand that, Why do you tell me that, and Are you telling me that. In addition to reflective responses of this type, our program should make note of certain "hot" words. If no or not are used in three responses, the "doctor" might ask:

Why are you being so negative?

Also, if a significant part of the session has elapsed without reference to mother or father, the doctor might say:

Tell me about your parents.

Our implementation of DOCTOR gives us some (but not all) of ELIZA's capabilities. The main procedure is shown below. It keeps count of the number of dialog segments and uses two subprocedures. The first, ANALYSIS, needs to accept a statement from the user and perform certain analyses on it. This procedure will use several global variables that must be initialized with the START command:

```
TO START
MAKE "NO 0
MAKE "FATHER 0
MAKE "MOTHER 0
MAKE "PREFIX [[TELL ME WHY] [I UNDERSTAND THAT] [WHY
    DO YOU TELL ME THAT] [ARE YOU TELLING ME THAT]]
CLEARTEXT
NICEPRINT [PLEASE TELL ME WHY YOU ARE HERE TODAY] 39 0
PRINT []
END
```

The **ANALYSIS** procedure has several tasks:

```
TO ANALYSIS
MAKE "USERINPUT SHIFT READLIST
IF MATCHP [NO NOT] :USERINPUT [MAKE "NO :NO + 1]
IF MEMBERP "FATHER :USERINPUT [MAKE "FATHER :FATHER
    + 1]
IF MEMBERP "MOTHER :USERINPUT [MAKE "MOTHER :MOTHER
    + 1]
END
```

This procedure uses two new operations that we have to define. The first of these, **SHIFT**, transforms a list into a list of words in which all the letters are uppercase. The recursive definition of this useful procedure is the following:

```
TO SHIFT :list
IF EMPTYP :list [OUTPUT []]
OUTPUT FPUT UPPERCASE FIRST :list SHIFT BUTFIRST :list
END
```

We can try this procedure by entering:

```
PRINT SHIFT [this is a test]
```

This will produce:

```
THIS IS A TEST
```

The reason we use a SHIFTed version of the user's input is to make word matching easier and to make the computer response always appear in uppercase letters.

The second new operation we used in ANALYSIS is MATCHP. This operation is similar to MEMBERP except that it will test for the occurrence of any of a list of elements in another list:

```
TO MATCHP :list1 :list2
IF EMPTYP :list1 [OUTPUT "FALSE]
IF MEMBERP FIRST :list1 :list2 [OUTPUT "TRUE]
OUTPUT MATCHP BUTFIRST :list1 :list2
END
```

We can test this procedure by entering

```
PRINT MATCHP [hello there] [there is a tavern in the town]
```

This will print TRUE on the screen because one of the words in the first list is contained in the second list. The equivalent of the MATCHP predicate is found in the language PILOT, where it is responsible for the creation of some interesting programs.

Because ANALYSIS accepts information from the user and updates the status of the "hot" words, we must now do the major work in our program: generating the response to the user's statement. To the extent that DOCTOR is intelligent, its intelligence must lie in the RESPONSE procedure. One version of this procedure follows:

```
TO RESPONSE :quest
IF EQUALP :quest 50 [NICEPRINT [THANK YOU FOR COMING
        TODAY. PERHAPS WE SHOULD CONTINUE AT A LATER
        TIME.] 38 0 THROW "TOPLEVEL]
IF :NO > 2 [PRINT [WHY ARE YOU BEING SO NEGATIVE?] MAKE
        "NO 0 STOP]
IF AND (:quest > 9) (AND (EQUALP :FATHER 0) (EQUALP
        :MOTHER 0)) [PRINT [TELL ME ABOUT YOUR PARENTS.]
        MAKE "FATHER 1 MAKE "MOTHER 1 STOP]
IF :FATHER > (:MOTHER + 5) [PRINT [TELL ME MORE ABOUT
        YOUR MOTHER.] STOP]
IF :MOTHER > (:FATHER + 5) [PRINT [TELL ME MORE ABOUT
        YOUR FATHER.] STOP]
IF EQUALP "WHY FIRST :USERINPUT [PRINT [SUPPOSE YOU
        TELL ME WHY.] STOP]
IF MATCHP [SAD UNHAPPY MISERABLE] :USERINPUT
        [NICEPRINT [I AM SORRY TO HEAR THAT - PLEASE GO ON.]
        38 0 STOP]
IF MEMBERP "AM :USERINPUT [NICEPRINT (SENTENCE RAND
        :PREFIX [YOU ARE] BUTFIRST MEMBER "AM :USERINPUT)
        38 0 STOP]
IF MEMBERP "I :USERINPUT [NICEPRINT (SENTENCE RAND
        :PREFIX [YOU] BUTFIRST "I :USERINPUT) 38 0 STOP]
IF MEMBERP "YOU :USERINPUT [PRINT [LET'S TALK ABOUT
        YOU, NOT ME.] STOP]
PRINT [TELL ME MORE.]
END
```

This procedure uses **RAND**, a procedure we developed in the previous chapter for picking items from a list randomly. For convenience, its listing is repeated here.

```
TO RAND :object
OUTPUT ITEM (1 + RANDOM COUNT :object) :object
END
```

The second new operation in **RESPONSE** is **MEMBER**. The function of this operation is to return a portion of a list starting with a target word. For example, if we were to enter

PRINT MEMBER "all [This is the time for all good men to come to
the aid of their country]

our screen would show:

all good men to come to the aid of their country

This is very useful in our DOCTOR program, because we want
to cleave a list around certain words and then use these list
parts to create a new response.

Before illustrating DOCTOR we should explore the form of
RESPONSE some more. In particular, this procedure is nothing
more than a set of conditional operations of the form:

IF :predicate (THEN) execute commands and return to the calling
procedure

From our previous experience with IF statements, we know
that the word THEN is implied in the version of Logo we are
using. All of these conditional statements return to the calling
procedure (by using the STOP command) except the first one.
The first statement checks for the end of the session (arbitrarily
set at 50 responses), and once this condition is met, execution
is THROWn to the top level of Logo ("TOPLEVEL). This set of
statements is hierarchical; in other words, the testing takes
place from the top downward. At the higher levels are our tests
for conditions relating to "hot" words, and if nothing else
works, the sentence TELL ME MORE is printed. In between
are the commands that reconstruct the user's input into a
reflected form from the computer. The structure and operation
of this procedure can be illustrated graphically by a tree in
which the search takes place from top to bottom in one pass.
As soon as one condition in the tree is satisfied, a result is
printed and the user goes on to the next statement.

Decision Tree for RESPONSE Procedure

```
                        50th quest?
                      yes |   no
        end program      3 no's?
                          yes |   no
            print message      no mention of parents?
                                 yes |   no
                 print message       lots of "father"?
                                      yes |   no
                     print message       lots of "mother"?
                                          yes |   no
                         print message       "why"?
                                              yes |   no
                             print message       sad words?
                                                  yes |   no
                                 print message       check for "am"?
                                                      yes |   no
                                     build response      check for "I"?
                                                          yes |   no
                                         build response      check for "you"?
                                                              yes |   no
                                             print message       print alternate
                                                                  message
```

To run our program a full 50 responses, we would enter

START DOCTOR 1

To test the program, I started partway through the session by entering

START DOCTOR 40

My dialog is shown below:

PLEASE TELL ME WHY YOU ARE HERE TODAY.
I don't like computers.
TELL ME ABOUT YOUR PARENTS.
Why should I tell you about my father?
SUPPOSE YOU TELL ME WHY.
You are asking too much.
LET'S TALK ABOUT YOU, NOT ME.
I just don't like computers.
TELL ME WHY YOU JUST DON'T LIKE COMPUTERS.
They are taking over the world.
TELL ME MORE.
I think they are evil.
ARE YOU TELLING ME THAT YOU THINK THEY ARE EVIL.
Yes.
TELL ME MORE.
They make me sad.
TELL ME MORE.
I am sad when I think about them.
I AM SORRY TO HEAR THAT - PLEASE GO ON.
Perhaps you are an exception to this.
LET'S TALK ABOUT YOU, NOT ME.
I think some programs might be good.
THANK YOU FOR COMING TODAY. PERHAPS WE
    SHOULD CONTINUE AT A LATER TIME.

As you can see, this brief dialog shows many of the branches used in our decision tree. The modest complexity of this tree creates the illusion that one is conversing with another person. It is tempting to compare this elaborate decision tree with the simple one used in TWENTY. In that program there were only three decisions to make: "Is the game over?", "Did the user enter a question?", and "Does the question end in a vowel?" DOCTOR is much more sophisticated in this regard. In fact, one measure of machine intelligence might be a measure of the size and complexity of the decision tree used in a program. By this measure, DOCTOR is far more intelligent than TWENTY.

But no matter how machine intelligence is measured, both of these programs are carefully crafted cheats. What was so interesting to Weizenbaum was the extent to which many users of ELIZA would treat this system as a truly intelligent program. Several health-care professionals, for example, thought that ELIZA would be useful for treating patients, and some people who had figured out how it worked would spend hours at the computer constructing carefully crafted statements to make certain that ELIZA didn't have trouble interpreting their statements.

It is as though some people wanted to believe that the artifact of machine intelligence was in some sense real.

As we look at even more intelligent programs, such as systems that model the behavior of experts in various fields, we can see the potential for tremendous personal and business benefits of artificial intelligence programs. For example, expert systems exist that help in tasks as simple as the choice of a good wine for dinner to tasks as complex as the prescription of an antibiotic for the treatment of rare bacteriological infections. Each of these expert systems makes extensive use of rules expressed in the form:

IF condition predicate is true THEN conclusion follows

For example, one rule for a wine adviser might be:

IF meal contains any of [lobster crab crayfish]
    AND sauce is strong
    THEN recommended wine is [white zinfandel]

(This is a hypothetical example, and you are free to disagree with my recommendation.)

Expert system software may contain many such rules—a few hundred or so, for example. The program can then query the user and lead him or her through a decision making process by asking questions, checking rules, and explaining its decision making process as it goes along. If the computer asks the user a question to check the applicability of a certain rule and the user doesn't know the answer, such programs can then ask other questions pertaining to other rules that might lead to an answer. Rather than operate with a strict hierarchy of rules (as does DOCTOR, for example), these programs have to search through all the rules in the system, and they can search for rules that would allow the system to make the best decision possible based on the information it has been given.

Clearly, programs of this sort are another notch above the sorts of artificial-intelligence programs described in this chapter, and yet they are capable of construction using languages like Logo. You may wish to explore other applications of artificial intelligence, and some of the references in the appendix will provide you with a rich assortment of projects to explore.

Our next topic is the use of Logo to build new computational objects.

VII.

Computing with Shapes and Sounds

The Nature and Representation of Computational Objects

Thus far in our explorations with Logo we have encountered several computational objects, the most traditional of which is the number. When we say we can compute with numbers, we are saying something everyone takes for granted. But, as with many other things we take for granted, it is to our advantage to explore this concept of number as object to see where it leads us.

Numbers have a readily identifiable symbolic representation: the symbols 0 1 2 3 4 5 6 7 8 9 and their combinations, such as 3.14159 and 385,600. They also have a set of operators that take one or several numbers and produce new numbers. These operators include the common commands SUM, DIFFERENCE etc., as well as the more esoteric operations such as SIN and SQRT. Number operators transform one or several numbers into another number or set of numbers (Logo's primitive number operators don't produce sets of numbers, but you can create new ones that do). Furthermore, we can classify Logo activities using numbers and their operators under the heading of arithmetic if we want. Clearly, it is to our advantage to have computational objects like numbers, because arithmetic is a very useful tool in computation.

But why are we going through this exercise of thinking of numbers as computational objects? The reason for this is that once we have identified the properties that make up any class of computational objects, we realize that we are free to create new ones of our own. The construction of a computational object lets us create new programs that use this object in a clear and unambiguous way.

In the context of this book, I will define two characteristics of computational objects: first, they have a symbolic representation and second, they have a set of operators that work with these representations to produce a desired result. In many cases, the result of the operation is to produce a new instance of the object, but in some cases the goal may be to produce a "side effect." Words and lists are two more examples of computational objects. The previous two chapters were filled with examples of the operators and types of computations that can be performed with these objects. As with numbers, the result of computing with words and lists is often the creation of more words and lists, although certain list operations produce words, and vice versa.

We have also encountered an object of a different type: the turtle. It has two major attributes: its position (given by **POS**) and its heading (given by **HEADING**). These combine to form the turtle's state. The various turtle operators (**FD, BK, LT, RT,** etc.) have the effect of changing this state. They can also produce the useful side effect of having lines drawn on the display. In fact, the turtle's side effects (creating lines) are normally more important to us than the numbers associated with the turtle's state.

The creation of a computational object involves nothing more than our thinking about a programming project in a certain way. To make a computational object, we need to define the object, pick a representation for the object that encompasses all its relevant attributes, pick the operators that we will use to interrogate and change the state of the object, and implement the representation and the operators.

We will choose to represent objects as data—typically lists. This is very different from the way objects are treated in languages like Smalltalk, where the object not only contains state information but also contains information regarding the kinds of messages (operators) it can use.

As a simple example of an object, let's consider a die with several numbered faces. A real (physical) die has several attributes: it has a color and a shape, a size, a certain number of faces, and certain numbers or markings on each face. Most importantly, it has one face that is "pointing up." The information on this face is the point count of the die, and it is very important information.

We can simulate as many of these attributes as we wish when creating our computational die; but there are several attributes that we don't need to have. We typically don't care about the color of the die, its shape, or its size. The only reason we might care about the die shape is to the extent that this shape information tells us which faces are favored over others. In our model, we will assume that all faces are equally likely.

Our representation of a die will be a list containing two elements: the number of the face that is pointing up and the number of faces on the die. We will make the arbitrary choice that the value of the die is the first element in the list, and the number of faces is the second:

[pointvalue faces]

The operations one can perform on a die are throwing it, reading its value, and counting its number of faces. We will create these operators, and we will create another die operation that lets us clone a new die that is an exact replica of an old one.

Our initial die object can be created simply by entering

MAKE ''DIE [1 6]

This gives us a die with six sides, side 1 of which is pointing upwards initially.

Creating the operator to give us the number of faces on the die is simple:

```
TO FACES :diename
OUTPUT LAST THING :diename
END
```

If we enter

```
PR FACES "DIE
```

6 will appear on the screen. Next we need to read the top face. We can do this easily:

```
TO READ :diename
OUTPUT FIRST THING :diename
END
```

If we now enter

```
PR READ "DIE
```

1 will appear on the screen, because that is how the die started out.

To toss the die we need to generate a random number between 1 and the number of faces on the die and modify the die object list to have this new value as its first element. This can be done with the following procedure:

```
TO TOSS :diename
MAKE :diename SENTENCE (1 + RANDOM LAST THING
    :diename) LAST THING :diename
END
```

Now if we enter

```
TOSS "DIE
PR READ "DIE
```

the number 5 might appear or some other number indicating that the die has been rolled to a new face. Finally, we should be able to clone a new die. The die-factory operator is very simple as well:

```
TO CLONE :old :new
MAKE :new THING :old
END
```

If we now enter

```
CLONE "DIE "NEWDIE
```

and then

```
PONS
```

(for Print Out NameS), two variables will appear in our work-space with the same values:

```
MAKE "NEWDIE [5 6]
MAKE "DIE [5 6]
```

We can now toss **NEWDIE** just as we tossed our original one, and we can create as many six-sided dice as we wish.

This example was intentionally kept simple to illustrate a way of defining and building a computational object and its operators. Our next project is a little more ambitious: the creation of a herd of turtles.

The Four-Turtle Problem

There is an interesting problem in mathematics associated with pursuit. Suppose four turtles are situated so that each one is at the corner of a square. The first turtle is to crawl towards the second turtle while the second crawls towards the third, the third towards the fourth, and the fourth towards the first. What paths will the turtles trace on the screen?

In order to solve this problem, it is helpful to have four turtles, each of which can be controlled independently of the others. Our solution to this problem will take advantage of the fact that our computer can do only one thing at a time, so we will take our "real" turtle and "time-share" it among four phantom turtles that we will create. Because the state of a turtle is given by its position and its heading, we can easily create a phantom turtle as a list of this information. For this particular problem we don't need the heading information (I will show why later), and we can thus define our turtles as a list of coordinates.

We will start our four turtles at the corners of a square with the following procedure:

```
TO SETUP
MAKE "TURTLE1 [60 60]
MAKE "TURTLE2 [60 -60]
MAKE "TURTLE3 [-60 -60]
MAKE "TURTLE4 [-60 60]
END
```

This defines and distributes our turtles clockwise around the square, starting at the upper right corner.

Next we must define the operation that will cause one turtle to move towards another one. This is done by setting our "real" turtle to the position of the turtle that is going to move, setting its heading towards the second turtle, and then moving it forward a small amount. Fortunately for us, Logo has a useful primitive operation, **TOWARDS**, that returns the heading needed to point the turtle towards any *x-y* coordinate on the screen. Our basic movement operation is then given by:

```
TO MOVETOWARDS :t1 :t2
PU SETPOS THING :t1
SETHEADING TOWARDS THING :t2
PD FD 5 PU
MAKE :t1 POS
END
```

This procedure moves the turtle t1 towards t2 by five units and makes the new value of the turtle state for t1 equal to its ending position. We would be more accurate if we moved the turtle by only one unit each time, but the resulting computation time for solving the problem would become quite long. Experiment with different turtle step sizes if you wish.

To see the operation of **MOVETOWARDS**, enter:


```
SETUP
REPEAT 10 [MOVETOWARDS TURTLE1 TURTLE3]
REPEAT 10 [MOVETOWARDS TURTLE1 TURTLE2]
```


This starts the turtle moving towards the lower left corner and then moves it towards the lower right corner:

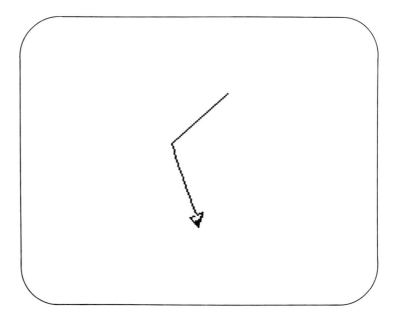

Now we are ready to create a new operator for the multiple turtles—one that will have them all chase each other:

```
TO CHASE
MOVETOWARDS "TURTLE1 "TURTLE2
MOVETOWARDS "TURTLE2 "TURTLE3
MOVETOWARDS "TURTLE3 "TURTLE4
MOVETOWARDS "TURTLE4 "TURTLE1
END
```

This operation will perform the chasing task given in the problem statement. To see the start of the solution to our original problem, enter

```
CS SETUP
REPEAT 5 [CHASE]
```

This procedure will show the first few steps of the solution on the screen. We will see the turtle hopping to its new position as it takes turns being each of the phantom turtles.

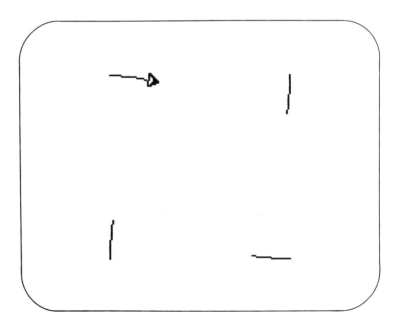

Finally, we can see the result of the continued chase by entering

REPEAT 25 [CHASE]

(If we hide the turtle the chase will go faster, and it is easier to see the final state of the chase in the center of the screen.)

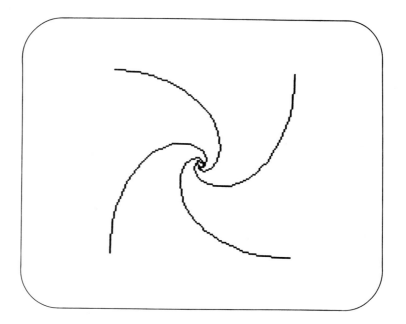

Suppose our conditions were different. For example, we might have the turtles start at the same locations, except instead have TURTLE1 chase TURTLE3, TURTLE3 chase TURTLE2, TURTLE2 chase TURTLE4, and TURTLE4 chase TURTLE1. We can accomplish this by editing CHASE as follows:

```
TO CHASE
MOVETOWARDS "TURTLE1 "TURTLE3
MOVETOWARDS "TURTLE3 "TURTLE2
MOVETOWARDS "TURTLE2 "TURTLE4
MOVETOWARDS "TURTLE4 "TURTLE1
END
```

If we now enter

```
CS SETUP
REPEAT 30 [CHASE]
```

we will see the following trajectories on the screen:

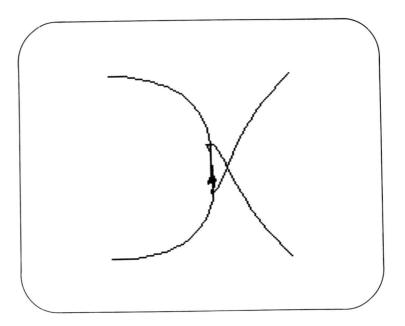

Notice that even though TURTLE4 is still chasing TURTLE1, it has a different trajectory because TURTLE1 is chasing TURTLE3 instead of TURTLE2.

So far our turtles have been programmed to chase each other. But just as we created an attraction operator (MOVE-TOWARDS), we might want to explore one that causes one turtle to move away from another one:

```
TO MOVEAWAY :t1 :t2
PU SETPOS THING :t1
SETHEADING 180 + TOWARDS THING :t2
PD FD 5 PU
MAKE :t1 POS
END
```

We can see the effect of this procedure by modifying our original version of CHASE to have TURTLE3 avoid TURTLE4.

```
TO CHASE
MOVETOWARDS "TURTLE1 "TURTLE2
MOVETOWARDS "TURTLE2 "TURTLE3
MOVEAWAY "TURTLE3 "TURTLE4
MOVETOWARDS "TURTLE4 "TURTLE1
END
```

Because TURTLE3 is going to avoid TURTLE4, we should alter SETUP to place TURTLE3 closer to TURTLE4 at the start of the chase:

```
TO SETUP
MAKE "TURTLE1 [60 60]
MAKE "TURTLE2 [60 −60]
MAKE "TURTLE3 [−50 50]
MAKE "TURTLE4 [−60 60]
END
```

Also, we need to let TURTLE3 move off the screen without wrapping around to the other side. This is accomplished by our issuing the primitive command WINDOW. If we now enter

CS WINDOW SETUP
REPEAT 30 [CHASE]

we will see the following display:

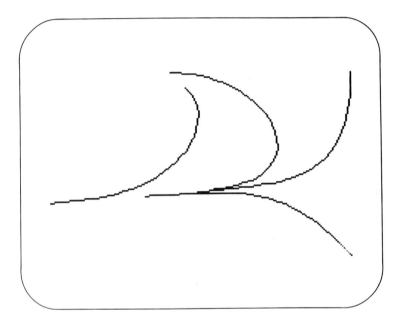

The net effect of having **TURTLE3** avoid **TURTLE4** is that it causes all the other turtles to chase after **TURTLE3**. By avoiding one turtle, **TURTLE3** has the appearance of being a leader!

Experiment some more with multiple turtles and different versions of **CHASE**. By changing the starting positions in **SETUP** and using different combinations of **MOVETOWARDS** and **MOVEAWAY** in **CHASE** you can create many interesting trajectories on the screen.

The Musical Score Object

As our next computational object, we will explore something a little more difficult: music.

We can create musical sounds with Logo by using the

TOOT primitive. TOOT plays a specified frequency tone for a specified duration. The form of the command is

TOOT :freq :duration

For example, if we enter

TOOT 440 60

we will hear the A above middle C for a duration of one second. If you are using an Apple IIc you may not hear the tone. You can adjust the volume of the internal speaker on the IIc with the volume control located on the left side of your computer. If your IIc is connected to a televsion set you can hear the tone through the television speaker instead of the internal speaker if you wish. The tone quality produced by TOOT isn't very good, but its quality is high enough for us to use it in exploring musical scores as computational objects.

Because the frequency input to TOOT is measured in Hertz (Hz), we can play notes from any scale we wish. If we want to play music in the equal-tempered chromatic scale we can create a set of lists containing the frequencies associated with each octave:

Note:	C	C#	D	D#	E	F	F#	G	G#	A	A#	B
MAKE "OCT1	[33	35	37	39	41	44	46	49	52	55	58	62]
MAKE "OCT2	[65	69	73	78	82	87	92	98	104	110	117	123]
MAKE "OCT3	[131	139	147	156	165	175	185	196	208	220	233	247]
MAKE "OCT4	[262	277	294	311	330	349	370	392	415	440	466	494]
MAKE "OCT5	[523	554	587	622	659	698	740	784	830	881	932	988]
MAKE "OCT6	[1047	1109	1176	1244	1319	1398	1480	1566	1663	1761	1864	1973]
MAKE "OCT7	[2095	2213	2346	2495	2637	2797	2959	3142	3327	3510	3743	3946]

We can choose the range of our instrument by combining several octaves through the use of the SENTENCE operation.

To test TOOT some more, here is a procedure that will play all the notes in an octave list for a fixed duration:

```
TO TOOTTEST :list
IF EMPTYP :list [STOP]
TOOT FIRST :list 10
TOOTTEST BUTFIRST :list
END
```

By entering

TOOTTEST :OCT1

we will hear the scale of notes in the first octave. If you enter

TOOTTEST (SE :OCT1 :OCT2 :OCT3 :OCT4 :OCT5 :OCT6 :OCT7)

we will hear the notes from all the octaves we created.

To play music with TOOT, one can select the notes to be played from the various octave lists using an operation like ITEM.

Now that we know how to produce musical sounds with Logo, computing with music ought not to be much harder than computing with words or turtles. As with our previous examples, we must decide what object we want to represent, and we must choose the operations we will want to perform on that object. The musical object we will explore is the score. We could have started with other objects—instruments, for example—but the musical score is a good choice, as we shall see.

A musical score is normally represented graphically, as with this fragment of a Bach minuet:

Minuet

This representation of music contains a lot of information. For example, it contains major information concerning the sequence of notes to be played and their relative durations. It also contains information on the tempo of the piece and its key. Some transcriptions include information germane to its performance on a particular instrument (finger position, bow direction, etc.).

Given that the object we want to represent is a musical score, we should now explore the operations we want to be able to perform on the score. We must first be able to compose or transcribe music to create the score. We also should be able to play the music back through our instrument (TOOT). Two other operations are very useful: the ability to transpose a score into a new key and the ability to change the tempo of the score. These four operations (composing, playing, transposing, and changing tempo) will define our starting set of music operators.

Given the limitations of our instrument (specifically that it can play a single tone with only one timbre or volume), our score can have a very simple representation: it will be composed of a list containing a list of notes to be played, an equally long list of durations for the notes, and a list containing the modifications of key and tempo:

[[notes] [durations] [modifications]]

The first two lists have a length determined by the length of the piece being played, and the last list consists of only two numbers (the transposition and tempo factor). Individual notes and durations will be represented by numbers. The reason for representing them in this way is that the note number can be used with a primitive like ITEM to pick a note from a list of frequencies. The duration number can be used directly with TOOT to pick the time for which a note will sound. A second advantage for using numbers to represent notes and durations is that transpositions can be performed simply by adding or subtracting a number from each element in the first list, and tempos can be changed by multiplying or dividing numbers in the second list by a fixed amount. The default modification list will have the elements [0 1] to indicate no transposition and the original tempo.

The COMPOSE operation has the function of accepting note and duration values from the keyboard and assembling these into a score:


```
TO COMPOSE :score
LOCAL [tempnotes temptimes temp]
MAKE "tempnotes []
MAKE "temptimes []
PRINT [Enter notes and durations. To end score enter 0 for
    duration.]
ADDNOTES
MAKE :score (LIST :tempnotes :temptimes [0 1])
END
```


This operation makes use of ADDNOTES to build the note and duration lists:

```
TO ADDNOTES
MAKE "temp READLIST
IF EQUALP LAST :temp 0 [STOP]
MAKE "tempnotes LPUT FIRST :temp :tempnotes
MAKE "temptimes LPUT LAST :temp :temptimes
ADDNOTES
END
```

In order to use **COMPOSE**, we need to have a scale of notes that defines the range of our instrument. The scale we will use is made from the notes contained in **OCT4** through **OCT6**. We can create this scale by entering

MAKE "SCALE (SE :OCT4 :OCT5 :OCT6)

If we now show the contents of **SCALE**, we will see the following list of frequencies:

[262 277 294 311 330 349 370 392 415 440 466 494 523 554 587 622
    659 698 740 784 830 881 932 988 1047 1109 1176 1244 1319
    1398 1480 1566 1663 1761 1864 1973]

The notes we will play are obtained by selecting one of the frequencies in this list. For this scale, the note numbers (and corresponding notes) are shown in the following figure:

Notes for scale made from
octaves 4, 5, and 6

note: 1 2 3 4 5 6   7 8   9 10 11 12 13 14 15 16 17 18

note: 19 20 21 22 23 24 25 26 27 28 29 30 31 32 33 34 35 36

When we use COMPOSE to create a score, we can refer to this figure to find the number corresponding to each note that is to be played. For example, let's create a score that corresponds to the fragment of the Bach minuet shown on page 161. Using the note values from SCALE, we can place the note numbers below each note in the original score as shown below.

Minuet

Allegretto   J. S. Bach

notes: 15 8 10 12 13 15 8   8 17 1315 17 19 20 8 8

notes: 13 15 13 12 10 12 13 12 10 8 7 8 10 12 8 12 10

notes: 15 8 10 12 13 15 8   8 17 1315 17 19 20 8 8

notes: 13 15 13 12 10 12 13 12 10 8 10 12 10 8 7 8

On close inspection, we can see that the first and third lines of this score are identical. This lets us save some time and energy by breaking the score into three units. The first and third lines will be held in the score MINA, the second line will be in MINB, and the last line will be in MINC. In order to use COMPOSE we must establish the duration values for each note. This is largely an arbitrary setting, because we will be able to change the tempo of a piece when it is played. Because note values tend to change by factors of two, we should choose a duration that is a power of two. I have arbitrarily chosen to represent a quarter note by a duration value of 32. This produces the duration values shown in the following table:

symbol	name	duration value
○	whole	128
♩ (half)	half	64
♩	quarter	32
♪	eighth	16
♬	sixteenth	8
♬	thirty-second	4

Finally we are able to enter our minuet into the computer. For example, to enter **MINA** we would type:

```
COMPOSE "MINA
15   32
8    16
10   16
12   16
13   16
15   32
8    32
8    32
17   32
13   16
15   16
17   16
19   16
20   32
8    32
8    32
0    0
```

As soon as we enter the last line, **MINA** will be defined. If we now enter

```
SHOW :MINA
```

the following list will appear on the screen:

```
[[15 8 10 12 13 15 8 8 17 13 15 17 19 20 8 8] [32 16 16 16 16 32 32
    32 32 16 16 16 16 32 32 32] [0 1]]
```

Of course, we didn't make the score **MINA** just so we could look at it. We need to be able to hear what it sounds like.

To play a score we need a procedure that reads the note list, adds the transposition value to each note, reads the correct frequencies from the SCALE list, and plays the frequencies for durations given by the values in the duration list divided by the tempo setting for the score. All this is accomplished with the following two procedures:

```
TO PLAY :score
P1 FIRST THING :score FIRST BUTFIRST THING :score LAST
    THING :score
END
```

```
TO P1 :notes :times :mods
IF EMPTYP :notes [STOP]
IF EQUALP FIRST :notes 0 [WAIT (FIRST :times) * (LAST :mods)]
    [TOOT ITEM (FIRST :notes) + (FIRST :mods) :SCALE (FIRST
    :times) * (LAST :mods)]
P1 BUTFIRST :notes BUTFIRST :times :mods
END
```

One of the features of PLAY is that it lets us use a note value of 0 to indicate a rest. When a 0 is encountered in the note list, it causes the computer to wait for the duration period before continuing to the next note.

```
PLAY "MINA
```

We should now hear a steady (but a bit slow) version of the first line of the minuet! Next, we can use COMPOSE to create MINB and MINC. Once we have created these scores, we can play the entire minuet fragment by entering:

```
PLAY "MINA PLAY "MINB PLAY "MINA PLAY "MINC
```

We will hear the entire piece played without any delays between the various segments.

As written, this piece moves a little too slowly. To speed it up just a bit we can change its tempo with the CHTEMPO operation:

```
TO CHTEMPO :score :step
LOCAL "temp
MAKE "temp LAST THING :SCORE
MAKE "temp LIST FIRST :temp (LAST :temp) / :step
MAKE :score LPUT :temp BUTLAST THING :score
END
```

This procedure places the value of step in the last position of the last list in the score.

We can hear the result of CHTEMPO speeding up our minuet by a factor of 1.5:

```
CHTEMP "MINA 1.5
CHTEMPO "MINB 1.5
CHTEMPO "MINC 1.5
PLAY "MINA PLAY "MINB PLAY "MINA PLAY "MINC
```

This is a more suitable tempo for this piece. Experiment with other tempos, but remember that each tempo change will modify the tempo that the score already has. For example, if we were to enter

```
CHTEMPO "MINA 2
```

we would be increasing the speed to *three* times its original value, because we already increased it by one and a half with the previous tempo change.

The remaining operation is one that lets us transpose a score to a new key. The TRANSPOSE operator looks somewhat similar to CHTEMPO, because it also has the task of modifying the contents of the last list in the score:

```
TO TRANSPOSE :score
LOCAL "temp
MAKE "temp LAST THING :SCORE
MAKE "temp LIST FIRST :temp :STEP LAST :temp
MAKE :score LPUT :temp BUTLAST THING :score
END
```

Now we can transpose our scores to any key we wish. For example, to transpose our minuet fragment up a fifth (so that the note C would now sound as G, for instance), we need to add 7 to each note value. We can do this by entering:

```
TRANSPOSE "MINA 7
TRANSPOSE "MINB 7
TRANSPOSE "MINC 7
```

When we play these scores, they will each have been raised by seven tones from their original values. To move them back to the key of G again, enter:

```
TRANSPOSE "MINA −7
TRANSPOSE "MINB −7
TRANSPOSE "MINC −7
```

This exercise in treating music as a computational object should make it easy to design new objects on our own. To explore the musical objects some more, you might want to build a system that lets you compose music that appears in traditional notation on the screen as it is played. The lists for notes and durations can be read by any other procedures you want to create, including graphic procedures that would place the properly shaped note at the correct location on the staff. Before long, you may be known as "Franz List"!

The Geometric Shape Object

For our last exploration of computational objects we will revert to the graphic world, but in a way that takes us beyond turtle to computation with complete geometric shapes.

What does it mean to compute with shapes? If we started with an arbitrary shape such as the one shown below, we could change its size, rotate it, and reflect it across the x- and y-axes. These are just a few of the operations we can perform on a two-dimensional shape.

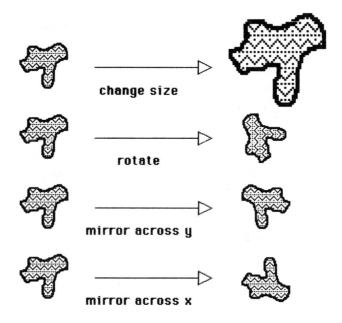

change size

rotate

mirror across y

mirror across x

Two-dimensional shapes can have many properties—boundary shape, color, texture, etc.—and all these properties obey certain mapping rules when the shape is operated upon. In the context of this chapter we will restrict our shape to a simple outline, although we will be able to expand the representation to include such parameters as color, filled or unfilled, etc. The operators we will create include those to change size, rotate, and reflect the shape across the x- or y-axis.

Before defining the representation for our shape object and its operators, we need to know how to rotate and mirror an image we have created with turtle graphics. We will start with a simple shape:

```
TO PATTERN
FD :S * 50 RT :A * 90
FD :S * 60 RT :A * 90
FD :S * 10 RT :A * 90
FD :S * 30 LT :A * 90
FD :S * 10 LT :A * 90
FD :S * 30 RT :A * 90
FD :S * 30 RT :A * 90
FD :S * 60 RT :A * 90
END
```

The variables S and A are explained in a moment. For now, set their values to 1:

```
MAKE "S 1
MAKE "A 1
```

If we now execute **PATTERN** this shape will appear on the screen:

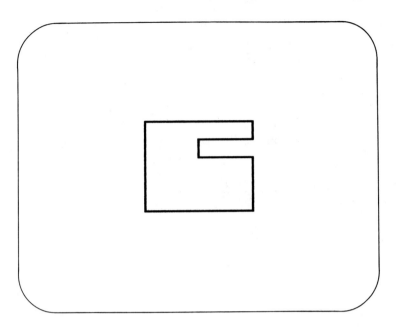

If we want to draw this shape in a rotated position we can enter

RT 30
PATTERN

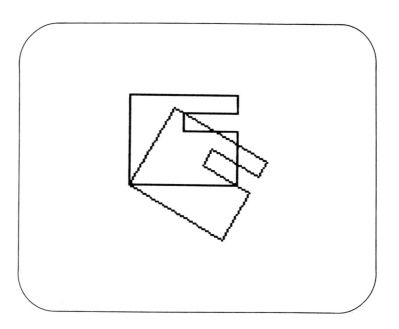

Next we need to see how we can create a mirror image of the shape reflected across the *y*-axis. For a clue on how to do this, draw the shape on a sheet of paper while holding a mirror vertically on the paper so you can see the reflected image. Notice that all the right turns have become left turns, and vice versa. To implement this mirror image, all we have to do is change the value of A to − 1:

```
CS PATTERN
MAKE "A −1
PATTERN
```

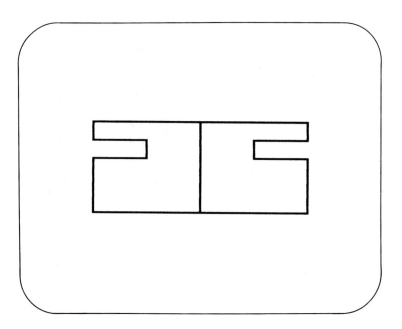

To flip the original image across the *x*-axis, we must make both S and A equal to − 1:

```
MAKE "A 1
CS PATTERN
MAKE "A −1
MAKE "S −1
PATTERN
```

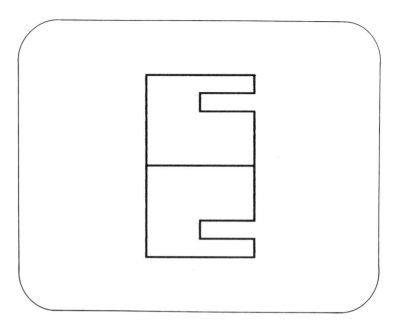

As we can see by looking at the PATTERN procedure, the pattern can be made larger by increasing the value of S.

Our shape object needs to have two parts: a procedurelike part that defines the basic shape of the object and a part containing information on rotation, scale, and mirroring. As with our previous objects, we will use a list of lists to represent our shapes. The shape-description list can be executed by the RUN command, and it can make use of the rotation, scale, and mirror data stored in the second list:

[[turtle commands] [orientation and size data]]

For example, we will illustrate computations using SHAPE1—a shape that is initialized with the following procedure:

```
TO SHAPEDEF
MAKE "SHAPE1 [[SETHEADING :rot * :refl FD :scale * 40 RT :refl *
    90 FD :scale * 30 RT :refl * 90 FD :scale * 10 RT :refl * 90 FD
    :scale * 20 LT :refl * 90 FD :scale * 30 RT :refl * 90 FD :scale *
    10 RT :refl * 90] [0 1 1]]
END
```

The reason for defining this list inside a procedure is to make it easy for us to recreate the original form of **SHAPE1** any time we want by entering

```
SHAPEDEF
```

One of the first operations we will need is one that stamps a copy of a shape on the screen. This procedure must extract the rotation, scale, and mirror parameters from the last list in the shape object and then use **RUN** to create a copy of the shape on the screen. The following procedure does this for us:

```
TO STAMP :shape
LOCAL [rot scale refl]
MAKE "rot FIRST LAST THING :shape
MAKE "scale FIRST BUTFIRST LAST THING :shape
MAKE "refl LAST LAST THING :shape
RUN FIRST THING :shape
END
```

To see the shape we have created, enter

```
SHAPEDEF
STAMP "SHAPE1
```

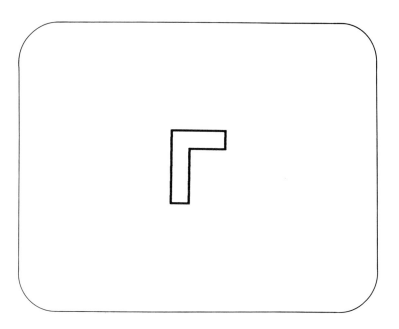

Next we should create an operator to change the size of our shape:

```
TO CHSIZE :shape :amt
LOCAL [rot scale refl]
MAKE "rot FIRST LAST THING :shape
MAKE "scale FIRST BUTFIRST LAST THING :shape
MAKE "refl LAST LAST THING :shape
MAKE "scale :scale * :amt
MAKE :shape LIST FIRST THING :shape (LIST :rot :scale :refl)
END
```

This procedure alters the scale parameter in the last list in the shape definition by multiplying it by the factor **amt**. To double the size of SHAPE1 we can enter

```
CHSIZE "SHAPE1 2
```

If we now enter

STAMP "SHAPE1

a large copy of the original shape will be added to the screen:

    The **ROTATE, MIRRORY,** and **MIRRORX** operators are similar to **CHSIZE** in that they each modify the appropriate parts of the last list in the shape representation:

```
TO ROTATE :shape :amt
LOCAL [rot scale refl]
MAKE "rot FIRST LAST THING :shape
MAKE "scale FIRST BUTFIRST LAST THING :shape
MAKE "refl LAST LAST THING :shape
MAKE "rot :rot + :amt
MAKE :shape LIST FIRST THING :shape (LIST :rot :scale :refl)
END
```

```
TO MIRRORY :shape
LOCAL [rot scale refl]
MAKE "rot FIRST LAST THING :shape
MAKE "scale FIRST BUTFIRST LAST THING :shape
MAKE "refl LAST LAST THING :shape
MAKE "refl :refl * ( −1)
MAKE :shape LIST FIRST THING :shape (LIST :rot :scale :refl)
END

TO MIRRORX :shape
LOCAL [rot scale refl]
MAKE "rot FIRST LAST THING :shape
MAKE "scale FIRST BUTFIRST LAST THING :shape
MAKE "refl LAST LAST THING :shape
MAKE "refl :refl * ( −1)
MAKE "scale :scale * ( −1)
MAKE :shape LIST FIRST THING :shape (LIST :rot :scale :refl)
END
```

To illustrate these operators, enter

```
CS STAMP "SHAPE1
ROTATE "SHAPE1 30
STAMP "SHAPE1
```

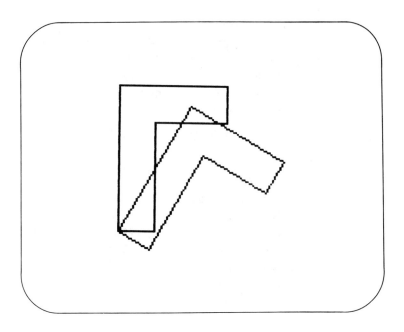

CS STAMP "SHAPE1
MIRRORY "SHAPE1
STAMP "SHAPE1

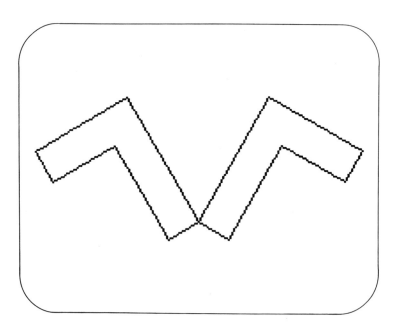

```
CS STAMP "SHAPE1
MIRRORX "SHAPE1
STAMP "SHAPE1
```

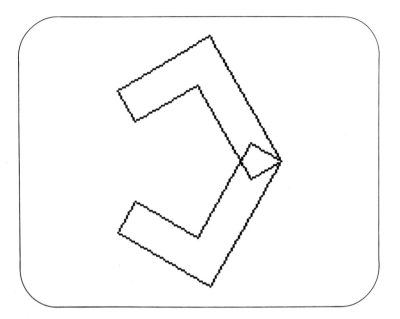

We can modify the shape object to include color and fill in-formation if we desire. Also, we can expand the operators to include one that will create a copy of the shape translated along an axis. In symmetry theory these translations are called glides. Also, as with our other shapes, we can clone copies using the **CLONE** procedure defined earlier in this chapter.

Now we move from the creation of our own computational objects to the creation of our own computer language!

VIII.

Lolly: A Knowledge Base Language You Create Yourself

By this time you have pretty well mastered Logo. For example, you know that Logo is far more than just a turtle-graphics language. You also know that Logo lets you add your own procedures to tailor the language to your own personal style.

In this chapter we use Logo to do something new: we are going to create our own programming language. In designing this language, I wanted it to have the following properties:

- It should be useful.
- It should be easy to implement.
- It should be easy to modify and extend the language.

Choosing a Language to Write

The first task in creating a new computer language is to decide just what kind of language to create. We could make a language like BASIC, but that wouldn't be very interesting. We could create a language like Logo, but that might be confusing, because we already have Logo.

The language we create should be able to work with information useful to us. Because we already have languages that do a good job at working with numbers, our language should work with other types of information.

One type of information that might be useful for a language to deal with is assertions such as the following:

John likes Mary.

Fred eats spinach.

Cows give milk.

Fish gotta' swim.

Birds gotta' fly.

Ol' man river, he jes' keeps rollin' along.

We call information of this form assertions rather than facts, because we can't very well expect the computer to establish the truthfulness of our statements, can we? After all, we could assert that birds have lips, but this doesn't make it a fact. If we were to decide to call assertions factoids to indicate that they aren't always true, then some people might want to call them falsettos, or something, because they aren't always false, either. This would immediately result in the formation of two opposing philosophical camps, each with their own newsletters, T-shirts, etc. The confusion would be horrendous, and most of us would quickly become bored with the whole mess and decide to watch a game on television instead. *Assertion*, on the other hand, has a nice, neutral tone to it, and will serve us just fine.

Well, this is an impressive start, because we have decided to build a language around the manipulation of information that is expressed in normal English sentences! (Note that the foregoing statement will end up being wrong, but as language designers, we are free to make bold claims of this sort until we actually start writing the language. That is where the compromises come in.)

Once we have created a set of assertions in the computer's memory (we will call this set the *knowledge base*), we need to decide what sorts of things we want to do with it. One thing we most certainly will want to do is interrogate our knowledge base. We will probably want to ask three types of questions. The first type will merely verify the existence of a particular relationship. A question of this sort is:

Do cows have wings?

We will also want our computer to answer questions such as:

Who killed Cock Robin?

In addition, we will want the computer to be able to describe the attributes of a particular object. For example, the command:

Describe dogs.

might produce:

Dogs are mammals.
Dogs like people.
John hates dogs.
Dogs eat too much.

Of course, our language must be able to do other things: to add new assertions, remove those we don't want, and perform other chores we will think up as we go along. If we do our job properly, we will be able to build our language incrementally, adding and modifying features as we use it.

I have decided to call this new language Lolly, because it sounds nice and because Lolly was what the Apple IIc computer was called prior to its public announcement. Just so you can be pleased with your programming skills, you should know that Lolly resembles a small part of another computer language called PROLOG, which is an artificial-intelligence language with some similarities to LISP that has been popular with European computer scientists for years. PROLOG is currently stimulating worldwide interest, especially in Japan. Japanese researchers are interested in PROLOG as a language to be used with the "Fifth Generation" computers—a breed of super computers that by comparison may make today's technology look as sophisticated as counting on one's fingers.

Representing Knowledge

Before we go about creating our language, we need to know what kind of objects we are going to use to represent our assertions inside the computer. Three types of data objects are at our disposal: numbers, words, and lists. Because assertions are sentences, it makes sense to represent them by lists.

What restrictions should our assertions have? If we wanted to be craftier than I think we should be at this point, we could let our lists be arbitrarily long. This would let us deal with assertions as simple as

[Pizza is good]

or as complex as

[Some philosophers think that Aristotle was pretty smart, but not as smart as some of the other Greeks]

To make Lolly work properly we will need to find the subjects and objects (and possibly verbs) in our assertions. To keep things simple, we will restrict ourselves to a straightforward syntactic structure in which our assertions are expressed as simple sentences in the form of

[subject verb object]

(This will be abbreviated **SVO**.) This is good for items like:

[Dogs have fleas]

But suppose we want our subject to have a full name—Fred de Needle, for example. Well, we can preserve our **SVO** format with a three-item list such as:

[[Fred de Needle] weaves cloth]

In this case, the subject is a list, and the verb and object are each words.

We will adopt the rule that all assertions will consist of lists containing three items. The first item in the list is the subject, the second is the verb, and third is the object. Some of the more philosophical among you may wonder if this would restrict us from including an assertion that

[[The Queen] rules England]

because the Queen is not a subject, but we will save debate on that topic for later.

The effort devoted to choosing the structure for our representation of knowledge in Lolly will pay off handsomely, because once this issue is resolved, it is possible to design the primitive commands our language will use.

Designing the Primitive Commands

Lolly is built from commands we create. We must first decide if Lolly commands should be *prefix* commands (like those in most of Logo), or *postfix* commands. Because

DO [people eat chicken]

reads better than

[People eat chicken] DO

we will opt for prefix commands. This choice lets us get away with a nice trick: we can build our language as an extension of Logo. The alternative is to write procedures that would accept an entire Lolly statement, search the statement for the command and the item the command works with, and *then* figure out how to execute all of this. Although this alternative might be a "purer" experience in language writing, I want us to create something that is immediately useful rather than merely pure.

Another advantage in our approach is that Lolly will have all of Logo at its disposal, which means we don't have to create commands for mundane chores that Logo handles perfectly well on its own. Also, this approach appeals to my sense of laziness.

To get Lolly off to a good start we need to provide the language with two types of commands: one that lets us create or modify the knowledge base and one that lets us interrogate the knowledge base we have created. Additional commands to handle disk storage, etc., aren't needed, because we can use the same commands we use with Logo. We will start with three commands of each type and know that we can always add more commands if we need them.

The three creation or modification commands with which we will start are START, ADD, and REMOVE. Of these three, START is the most dangerous. When this command is given, the existing knowledge base is erased and Lolly is readied to start with a new base of information. Because of the irreversible nature of START, we should require that the user confirm his or her intention to use the command before it performs its chore.

The ADD and REMOVE commands operate in opposite fashion to each other. When the computer receives a command such as

ADD [[Jim Chu] runs races]

this assertion is added to the knowledge base. We can do this by first checking the assertion to be sure it is the correct length. Next, we will bind it to a variable named S*n* where *n* is a number indicating which assertion this is in the knowledge base. For example, if our assertion is S4, it is the fourth assertion in the knowledge base. The variable name (e.g., S4) is then added to a list called SENTENCE. There are several reasons for having a list of valid sentence names. One of these is that the length of the SENTENCE list is equal to the number of assertions presently in the knowledge base. When we create S4, we must let Lolly know that the next name will be S5, etc. If we denote the sentence number by N, then the ADD command can increase this value to N + 1 before it finishes.

If we enter the command

REMOVE [Dogs have fleas]

we want the assertion

[Dogs have fleas]

to be removed from the knowledge base. We will do this by searching through all the sentences (S1, S2, S3, etc.) until we find the one containing the desired relationship. We will then erase that sentence from the knowledge base and erase its name (S16, for example) from the SENTENCE list.

In summary, ADD lets us add new assertions to the knowledge base, REMOVE lets us remove assertions we don't want, and START lets us start creating a knowledge base from scratch.

Of course, none of this would be of any use if we weren't going to *interrogate* our knowledge base. The three interrogation commands we will create are DOES (or DO) ASK, and DESCRIBE. The DOES or DO command simply verifies the existence of an assertion in the knowledge base. If we enter

DOES [John like anchovies]

and this assertion is in the knowledge base, the computer will respond with

Yes

Otherwise it will respond with

No answer

Because you are writing Lolly yourself, you could have other responses such as Yup, True, You just ain't 'a whistlin' Dixie, or whatever. Similarly, No answer could be replaced by False, Negatory, good buddy!, or whatever else your fertile mind might devise.

In operation, there is no difference between DO and DOES. The reason for having both is so we don't have to enter

DOES [flowers smell nice]

and can instead enter a more English-like query such as

DO [flowers smell nice]

This command operates by simply looking to see if the assertion appearing after DO or DOES is presently in the knowledge base. If it is, the affirmative answer is printed, and if it isn't, the negative answer is printed instead.

The command ASK is trickier to implement than DO, but then again, it is also very powerful. With this command you can enter questions such as

ASK [What is yellow]

and the computer will search its knowledge base for all assertions that contain the words

is yellow

and will then print the subjects of these assertions:

Answer is canary
Answer is Acacia flower
Answer is egg yolk
No (more) answers.

   If there are no assertions that satisfy the query, the response

No (more) answers

will be printed.

   In an effort to make Lolly as English-like as possible, we will want to accept any of the interrogative pronouns—who, what, where, which, etc. Also, we will want to be able to use pronouns in either the subject or object position. This lets us enter

ASK [[Sue Ellen] shot whom]

as well as

ASK [Who shot J.R.]

   In operation, the **ASK** command first needs to establish that there is a pronoun in the query. After all,

ASK [John eats anchovies]

doesn't make any sense—especially because I happen to know that he hates anchovies, but that is another story. If there is no acceptable pronoun in the query, we may want to have the system respond with an appropriate error message:

Please try again with the proper format.

or

I can't find the pronoun in your query.

or

Can't you type better bit-breath?

Once a pronoun is found, we must search either the verb-object, or the subject-verb portion of the assertions in the knowledge base for a match against the corresponding part of our query. Each time a match is found, the corresponding subject (or object) is printed on the screen. Once the end of the knowledge base has been reached, the response

No (more) answers.

is printed on the screen.

The last Lolly command we will design is the DESCRIBE command. It takes a subject, verb, or object as its input and causes Lolly to list every relationship that incorporates this item. For example, the command

DESCRIBE [Eileen Dover]

might result in Lolly's printing the following:

[Eileen Dover] is pretty
[Eileen Dover] is silly
Fred likes [Eileen Dover]
No (more) answers.

DESCRIBE has another powerful function. If we enter the command

DESCRIBE ''ALL

a list of the entire knowledge base will appear on the screen.

DESCRIBE is a fairly easy command to implement. If the target item is ALL, it lists the entire knowledge base; otherwise it searches through the knowledge base to see if the target word or list appears in any position in any of the assertions. If it does, the corresponding assertion is displayed on the screen. If the end of the knowledge base is reached or no matches can be found, the message

No (more) answers.

will be printed on the screen.

Well, I have described the start of an interesting language. Next we will turn this description into a set of Logo procedures and try it out!

Implementation of the Commands

As was mentioned before, the use of a prefix notation for Lolly lets us implement the language as a set of Logo procedures rather than as a set of lists that must be parsed, interpreted, and then executed—a much more time-consuming task.

To minimize the confusion attendant in the creation of interesting procedures, the Lolly commands will be implemented in the order in which they were described.

The Lolly knowledge base must start with two global variables, the list of existing assertions (SENTENCE), and the number of the next assertion to be named (N). To begin at the beginning, SENTENCE will be empty, and N will equal 1:

```
MAKE "SENTENCE []
MAKE "N 1
```

Another global variable will be used to hold a list of pronouns. The first Lolly primitive we will construct is START:

```
TO START
PR [This command will erase your knowledge]
PR [base. Enter 'Y' to confirm.]
IF EQUALP UPPERCASE READCHAR "Y [CLEANUP] [PR [No
    changes made.] PR []]
END
```

When this command is executed, the user is given the chance to abort the command or accept it. Use of the Logo UPPERCASE operation on the character read from the keyboard will let either y or Y be accepted as the yes response. Any other character will abort this command.

If the Y key is pressed, Logo will then execute the CLEANUP procedure:

```
TO CLEANUP
ERN :SENTENCE
MAKE "SENTENCE []
MAKE "N 1
MAKE "PRONOUNS [WHO WHAT WHICH WHERE WHOM WHEN]
END
```

This command erases all the variables named in the SENTENCE list through the use of the Logo ERN (ERase Names) command and resets SENTENCE and N to their initial values.

The next Lolly command to be created is the one that lets us add new assertions to the knowledge base:

```
TO ADD :assert
IF NOT LISTP :assert [PR [This assertion is in the wrong form.]
    STOP]
IF NOT EQUALP LENGTH :assert 3 [PR [This assertion is the
    wrong length.] STOP]
MAKE "item WORD "S :N
MAKE :item :assert
MAKE "SENTENCE LPUT :item :SENTENCE
MAKE "N :N + 1
END
```

This command first performs some tests on the proposed assertion to be sure it is in the correct form. Remember that we want our assertion to be a list containing three items ([subject verb object]). First we will test to be sure that the proposed assertion is a list. Otherwise, the system might accept

ADD "rok

because rok has three elements (r, o, and k). Next, we test to be sure the assertion has only three elements. This keeps us from accidentally accepting assertions like

[Cows swim]
[Fred likes Nancy too]

Once this bit of checking is finished, we make a word consisting of S followed by the present value of N and bind the assertion to this name. Notice that we do this by making the contents of item (:item) the name of the assertion rather than binding the assertion to the word "item itself. Once this is done, the name (e.g., S26) is appended to the SENTENCE list and the value of N is increased by 1.

ADD is built from Logo primitives, except for the command LENGTH that determines the length of a list or word:

```
TO LENGTH :item
IF EMPTYP :item [OUTPUT 0]
OUTPUT 1 + LENGTH BUTFIRST :item
END
```

(The Logo primitive COUNT can be used instead of LENGTH.)

The next Lolly primitive to be defined is the REMOVE command that lets us take an assertion out of our knowledge base:

```
TO REMOVE :assert
MAKE "item EXISTING :assert :SENTENCE
IF EQUALP :item "none [PR SENTENCE :assert [was not found]
    STOP]
ERN :item
MAKE "SENTENCE CONDENSED :item :SENTENCE
PR :assert
PR [has been removed.]
PR []
END
```

REMOVE first uses the EXISTING operation to find the name of the assertion to be removed. (This operation is described below.) If the assertion is not found in the knowledge base, a message is printed and REMOVE is aborted. Once the assertion name has been located, the assertion is erased and its name is removed from the SENTENCE list through the use of the CONDENSED command.

The EXISTING operation is shown here:

```
TO EXISTING :list1 :list2
IF EMPTYP :list2 [OUTPUT "none]
IF EQUALP :list1 THING FIRST :list2 [OUTPUT FIRST :list2]
OUTPUT EXISTING :list1 BUTFIRST :list2
END
```

This operation searches for the existence of list1 in a collection of lists whose names are stored in list2. It performs the search recursively by checking to see if list1 is the contents of the first name in list2 and then repeating this search with a new list2 from which the first element has been removed. If no match is found, the word **none** is returned to the calling command, otherwise the name of the variable holding the desired list is returned.

The **CONDENSED** operation outputs a list from which a chosen item has been removed:

```
TO CONDENSED :item :list
IF EQUALP :item FIRST :list [OUTPUT BUTFIRST :list]
OUTPUT CONDENSED :item LPUT FIRST :list BUTFIRST :list
END
```

This operation checks to see if the item is at the front of the list. If it is, the procedure outputs all but the first element of the list; otherwise it recursively repeats this test on a rotated list in which the first element gets moved to the end of the list each time. Given the manner in which this operation has been written, it is essential that the desired item exists in the list, or the search will continue forever! Another characteristic of this procedure is that the condensed list will have its elements rotated from the original list. Because Lolly doesn't make any use of the order in which information is added to the knowledge base, this trait doesn't matter to us. As a programming challenge, you may wish to create a new version of **CONDENSED** that preserves the original order in the list.

Now that we have created the commands to let us build and modify our knowledge base, we are ready to implement the commands that let us interrogate our base of information.

The first Lolly command of this type is the **DOES** command:

```
TO DOES :assert
PR FIND :assert :SENTENCE
PR []
END
```

This command checks to see if the assertion resides anywhere in the knowledge base. It performs this task with the aid of the FIND operation:

```
TO FIND :list1 :list2
IF EMPTYP :list2 [OUTPUT [No answer.]]
IF EQUALP :list1 THING FIRST :list2 [OUTPUT [Yes.]]
OUTPUT FIND :list1 BUTFIRST :list2
END
```

FIND looks to see if the content of list1 is the same as that in the first variable listed in list2. If it is, the word Yes is returned to the calling command. Otherwise, this operation is repeated recursively on the remainder of list2 until a match is found, or until list2 is empty.

As was mentioned before, we need a plural form of the DOES query, which is quite easy to create:

```
TO DO :assert
DOES :assert
END
```

The ASK command locates and prints the subjects or objects that correspond to the pronoun part of the query:

```
TO ASK :query
IF MEMBERP SHIFT FIRST :query :PRONOUNS [FINDFIRST
    BUTFIRST :query :SENTENCE]
IF MEMBERP SHIFT LAST :query :PRONOUNS [FINDLAST
    BUTLAST :query :SENTENCE]
PR [No (more) answers.]
PR []
END
```

The **SHIFT** operation produces an uppercase version of any word or list. We need this because subjects and objects are not always likely to be words.

```
TO SHIFT :obj
IF WORDP :obj [OUTPUT UPPERCASE :obj]
IF EMPTYP :obj [OUTPUT []]
OUTPUT FPUT UPPERCASE FIRST :obj SHIFT BUTFIRST :obj
END
```

In operation, **ASK** splits the task into one of two subtasks, depending on whether the pronoun is in the subject or object position. If it appears in the subject position, all instances of the verb-object portion of the query are located in the knowledge base using the **FINDFIRST** command:

```
TO FINDFIRST :list1 :list2
IF EMPTYP :list2 [STOP]
MAKE "assert THING FIRST :list2
IF EQUALP :list1 BUTFIRST :assert [PR SENTENCE [Answer is]
    FIRST :assert]
FINDFIRST :list1 BUTFIRST :list2
END
```

This command prints the subjects of all assertions that contain the contents of list1 in the verb-object position. The recursive operation of this command is similar to that used in **EXISTING**.

If the pronoun in the **ASK** query is in the object position, then all instances of the subject-verb portion of the query are located in the knowledge base using the **FINDLAST** command:

```
TO FINDLAST :list1 :list2
IF EMPTYP :list2 [STOP]
MAKE :assert THING FIRST :list2
IF EQUALP :list1 BUTLAST :assert [PR SENTENCE [Answer is]
    LAST :assert]
FINDLAST :list1 BUTFIRST :list2
END
```

This command prints the objects of all assertions that contain the contents of list1 in the subject-verb position.

The last Lolly command we will create for the moment is the DESCRIBE command. It will list all the assertions containing a specified item or all the assertions in the knowledge base if the target item is the word All:

```
TO DESCRIBE :item
IF EQUALP SHIFT :item "ALL [LISTALL :SENTENCE STOP]
LISTPART :item :SENTENCE
END
```

DESCRIBE uses one of two subprocedures, depending on whether part or all of the knowledge base is to be listed. LISTALL simply lists the contents of all variables whose names are in a list:

```
TO LISTALL :list
IF EMPTYP :list [PR [No (more) answers.] PR [] STOP]
PR THING FIRST :list
LISTALL BUTFIRST :list
END
```

LISTPART is similar to LISTALL in its function, expect that it prints only the result if the target item is contained in the variable's contents:

```
TO LISTPART :item :list
IF EMPTYP :list [PR [No (more) answers.] PR [] STOP]
IF MEMBERP :item THING FIRST :list [PR THING FIRST :list]
LISTPART :item BUTFIRST :list
END
```

This set of procedures defines the beginning of our new language called Lolly. The next step is to test our creation to see how it performs.

Testing the Language

The best way to test any of our programming efforts is to present our procedures with both expected and unexpected responses. This is what we will do for Lolly. But before we do any experiments with our creation, we must be sure to save our workspace on the disk. Once we have done this, we are ready to start experimenting.

If you are using a monochrome monitor with your computer system, you might want to run Lolly with the 80-column display mode by entering:

```
SETWIDTH 80
CLEARTEXT
```

Next, enter:

```
START
```

You will see the message:

This command will erase your knowledge
base. Enter 'Y' to confirm.

Run this procedure a few times with various responses to be sure it works properly. Our next task is to add some items to our knowledge base. Start by entering

```
ADD [birds have lips]
```

and notice that this entry has been accepted by Lolly. Next, enter

```
ADD [dogs fly]
```

The system should respond with the following message:

This assertion is the wrong length.

Now enter

ADD "abc

and notice that Lolly rejects this entry as well.

Our next task is to create a sample knowledge base, so we should enter a few more assertions, such as:

ADD [cows have wings]
ADD [dogs can fly]
ADD [dogs eat spinach]
ADD [birds use [charge cards]]
ADD [[Charles Dickens] wrote [Tale of Two Cities]]
ADD [dogs run corporations]
ADD [ducks have [bad breath]]
ADD [ducks are birds]
ADD [John likes dogs]
ADD [dogs have fleas]
ADD [mares eat oats]
ADD [does eat oats]
ADD [cows [jump over] moons]

Each of these assertions should be accepted without any problem. Notice that we have created assertions in a variety of forms. We have examples that use lists and words in each of the three (subject-verb-object) positions. To see a list of the assertions accepted into the knowledge base, enter

DESCRIBE "all

and they will be listed on the screen. If you wish to have a copy of your knowledge base printed on the printer instead, enter

DRIBBLE 1 DESCRIBE "all NODRIBBLE

So far we know that START, ADD, and DESCRIBE all work properly. (If your copies don't work, check your procedures against the listings to see the source of the problem.) Next we will test our ability to remove an assertion from the knowledge base. To do this, enter

REMOVE [[Charles Dickens] wrote [tale of two cities]]

This should produce the message:

[Charles Dickens] wrote [tale of two cities] was not found

The reason we see this message is that our version of Lolly is sensitive to whether our assertions use uppercase or lowercase letters. In other words, Dog is treated differently from dog, and Tale is not equal to tale. Of course, our Lolly primitives are case insensitive because they are Logo procedures. Ask, ask, and aSK all refer to the same procedure. We can make searches of the knowledge base case-insensitive if you like, but we should be sure that this won't create more problems. For example, if we want to distinguish between Rose as a woman's name and rose as a flower, case insensitivity will not help you one bit.

In our form of the language, assertions must be typed the same way each time. This is a result of our choice in creating procedures, not a limitation of Logo.

And so to continue with our removal experience we need to type the assertion in its correct form. The easiest way to do this is to display the previously typed line by pressing **CTRL R** (to Recall the last line) and to edit the line to read as follows:

REMOVE [[Charles Dickens] wrote [Tale of Two Cities]]

Now the message

[Charles Dickens] wrote [Tale of Two Cities]
has been removed

will appear on the screen. If we list the assertions we will see that this one no longer appears in the knowledge base. We will also notice that the assertions are in a new order, as was explained when the writing of the REMOVE procedure was described.

Next we should check out the rest of the DESCRIBE primitive. If we enter

DESCRIBE ''ducks

we will see on the screen:

ducks have [bad breath]
ducks are birds
No (more) answers.

If we enter

DESCRIBE ''dogs

the word **dogs** will be found in both the subject and object positions:

dogs run corporations
John likes dogs
dogs have fleas
dogs can fly
dogs eat spinach
No (more) answers.

To test **DESCRIBE** for searches in the verb position, enter

DESCRIBE ''have

and we will see:

ducks have [bad breath]
dogs have fleas
birds have lips
cows have wings
No (more) answers.

To test the **DO** (or **DOES**) primitive, enter

DO [birds have lips]

and

Yes.

will appear on the screen. If we now enter

DOES [John like dogs]

the response

No answer.

will appear. The reason for this response is that the assertion was added as

[John likes dogs]

and Lolly "thinks" that like and likes are different, which shows that Lolly is not completely like English. As with case insensitivity, we can modify the primitives to look for "person-sensitive" verbs and to adjust its responses accordingly. This is less trivial than it might appear at first, but it is a good chance to show why computers generally have a hard time dealing with unrestricted natural language.

Rather than go through this effort, we can simply enter

DOES [John likes dogs]

and be satisfied when

Yes.

appears on the screen!

The remaining primitive to test is ASK, which can use a query containing a pronoun in either the subject or verb position. For example,

ASK [what have wings]

produces

Answer is cows
No (more) answers.

and

ASK [John likes what]

produces

Answer is dogs
No (more) answers.

    This test of our Lolly primitives shows us a few of the things this language can do. In the next chapter we put Lolly to work for us.

IX.

Programming in Lolly—Using Your Own Creation

Even though Lolly is a very primitive start at the development of a computer language, there are lots of things for which it can be used. We will explore a few of these applications in this chapter and discuss ways that you might want to expand Lolly to make it even more useful.

Personal Databases

Each of us has a wealth of information that is best recalled through the use of a database. To take a business application, for example, we might start with a personnel record system. Such a system works with information regarding the employees of a company, when they were hired, for whom they work, their title, etc. In a traditional database system we might create a data record for each employee consisting of several fields. Each of these fields would have a specific piece of information (title, salary, etc.). The problem with fixed-length records of this sort is that they make it hard to add new types of information that pertains to only a few employees. For example, if you want to indicate which employees are board members of the company, it would be silly to add a board member field to each record just to accommodate the three or four employees who are affected. With Lolly we can build as little or as much information as we want regarding each employee without affecting the form of any other items in the database.

For example, consider a Lolly knowledge base consisting of the following information:

ADD [[I. Scott Tugo] is president]
ADD [[I. Scott Tugo] [was hired] [May 15, 1981]]
ADD [[I. Scott Tugo] [works for] [the board]]
ADD [[Phil O'Dendron] is [v.p. finance]]
ADD [[Phil O'Dendron] [was hired] [June 22, 1982]]
ADD [[Phil O'Dendron] [works for] [I. Scott Tugo]]
ADD [[Sally Forth] is accountant]
ADD [[Sally Forth] [was hired] [May 20, 1981]]
ADD [[Sally Forth] [works for] [Phil O'Dendron]]
ADD [[Gene S. Pieces] is [v.p. operations]]
ADD [[Gene S. Pieces] [was hired] [July 17, 1984]]
ADD [[Gene S. Pieces] [works for] [I. Scott Tugo]]
ADD [[Robin deCradle] is [v.p. engineering]]
ADD [[Robin deCradle] [was hired] [Oct. 28, 1983]]
ADD [[Robin deCradle] [works for] [I. Scott Tugo]]
ADD [[Shanda Lear] is secretary]
ADD [[Shanda Lear] [was hired] [April 25, 1982]]
ADD [[Shanda Lear] [works for] [I. Scott Tugo]]
ADD [[Storm deBeaches] is secretary]
ADD [[Storm deBeaches] [was hired] [Aug. 7, 1983]]
ADD [[Storm deBeaches] [works for] [Robin deCradle]]
ADD [[Storm deBeaches] [works for] [Phil O'Dendron]]
ADD [[Storm deBeaches] [works for] [Gene S. Pieces]]

The list for most companies would obviously be much larger, but this set of entries will illustrate the system. For example, we can retrieve all kinds of useful information from this knowledge base. (Queries are shown as they appear on the screen.)

?Ask [who is president]

Answer is I. Scott Tugo
No (more) answers.

?Ask [who [works for] [I. Scott Tugo]]

Answer is Phil O'Dendron
Answer is Gene S. Pieces
Answer is Robin deCradle
Answer is Shanda Lear
No (more) answers.

?Ask [[Robin deCradle] is what]

Answer is secretary
No (more) answers.

?Describe [I. Scott Tugo]

[I. Scott Tugo] is president
[I. Scott Tugo] [was hired] [May 15, 1981]
[I. Scott Tugo] [works for] [the board]
[Phil O'Dendron] [works for] [I. Scott Tugo]
[Gene S. Pieces] [works for] [I. Scott Tugo]
[Robin deCradle] [works for] [I. Scott Tugo]
[Shanda Lear] [works for] [I. Scott Tugo]
No (more) answers.

Of course, businesses are not alone in their need to store and retrieve information. Each of us has a collection of books, records, tapes, or some other entity that we might want to have stored on the computer for applications as diverse as an insurance inventory to finding out who sang what song. For example, some of the books listed in appendix 4 were stored in a Lolly knowledge base using several pieces of information:

ADD [[S. Papert] wrote Mindstorms]
ADD [Mindstorms [appeared in] 1980]
ADD [Mindstorms features philosophy]
ADD [[Basic Books] published Mindstorms]

Once the bibliographic data base was complete I could find all the books I had on a certain topic by entering

ASK [Which features recursion]

and the computer would respond with:

Answer is Goedel, Escher, Bach
Answer is The Fractal Geometry of Nature
Answer is Inversions
No (more) answers.

Similarly, all the books published in a given year can be found:

?ASK [What [appeared in] [1981]
Answer is Turtle Geometry
Answer is Inversions
No (more) answers.

Even if one doesn't have a library to maintain, Lolly can be used effectively as a family to-do list:

ADD [Bob call plumber]
ADD [Ann clean room]
ADD [Ed wash car]
ADD [Sue fix computer]

Each person can find his or her chores by entering, for example,

DESCRIBE "Bob

for which the computer might print:

Bob call plumber
Bob paint bathroom
Bob clean pool
Bob buy groceries
Bob watch TV
Bob go sleep
No (more) answers.

As each chore is finished it can be removed from the knowledge base with the REMOVE command:

REMOVE [Bob go sleep]

The fairly unrestricted nature of Lolly makes it suitable for many novel applications.

Adding Arithmetic to Lolly

From the outset we designed Lolly for nonmath applications; yet we can view mathematics as a database activity by providing Lolly with a set of assertions pertaining to number facts:

ADD [[0 + 1] = 1]
ADD [[1 + 1] = 2]
ADD [[2 + 1] = 3]
ADD [[3 + 1] = 4]
.

.

.

If we were able to stuff a large number of such assertions into the computer (it will hold about a hundred or so), we could solve a problem by entering

ASK [[3 + 4] = what]

Answer is 7
No (more) answers.

There are two things to notice about this method of performing computations. First, it isn't very smart, because the computer isn't actually performing the operation of addition but is just looking for the appropriate number fact. Second, Lolly is performing this task the way we were taught to do it. The whole reason we were forced as children to memorize our math tables was so we could solve simple math problems from memory without having to perform the computation directly. Yes, Lolly is "stupid" in its way of doing math—just like us!

In fact, we can give this method of addition a name: CADET. This stands for **C**an't **A**dd; **D**oesn't **E**ven **T**ry.

The most cumbersome part of CADET is getting the facts into the system in the first place. Whereas we are willing to take several years to do this with humans, we can speed up the process quite a bit for the computer by creating a procedure to add new number facts to Lolly's base of knowledge. For example:

```
TO ADDFACTS :num1 :num2
IF :num2 < 0 [STOP]
ADD (LIST (LIST :num1 "+ :num2) "= (:num1 + :num2))
ADDFACTS :num1 :num2 − 1
END
```

To create a set of addition assertions in Lolly's knowledge base, clear the existing data with the **START** command and then enter

```
ADDFACTS 0  9
ADDFACTS 1  9
ADDFACTS 2  9
ADDFACTS 3  9
ADDFACTS 4  9
ADDFACTS 5  9
ADDFACTS 6  9
ADDFACTS 7  9
ADDFACTS 8  9
ADDFACTS 9  9
```

Once we have created this set of assertions we can ask "normal" questions such as:

ASK [[4 + 5] = what]

Answer is 9
No (more) answers.

We can also ask questions that are not normally allowed with calculators, such as:

ASK [What = 6]

Answer is 0 + 6
Answer is 1 + 5
Answer is 2 + 4
Answer is 3 + 3
Answer is 4 + 2
Answer is 5 + 1
Answer is 6 + 0
No (more) answers.

The fact that we can perform computations using either the answer or the problem makes Lolly's arithmetic very different from Logo's. In this regard Lolly is similar to other languages such as PROLOG or SOLO.

Adding a Shell to Lolly

So far we have been executing all of Lolly's primitives directly from Logo. Another choice available to us is the execution of our Lolly procedures from a shell. The function of a shell is to accept our commands and analyze them before they are executed. For example, we could build a shell for Lolly that only allows the execution of Lolly procedures and does not allow any of Logo's primitives to be used directly.

The shell shown below uses an asterisk instead of Logo's question-mark prompt:

```
TO LOLLY
TYPE "*
MAKE "COMMAND RL
IF MEMBERP SHIFT FIRST :COMMAND [ADD DO DOES
    DESCRIBE ASK REMOVE START] [RUN :COMMAND] [PRINT
    SE [I don't know how to] FIRST :COMMAND]
LOLLY
END
```

If we enter

LOLLY

an asterisk will appear on the screen instead of a question mark. If we start by entering a traditional Logo command that would mess up Lolly's text screen, such as

CS

the screen will then display:

I don't know how to CS

But if we enter a good Lolly command such as

ADD [[Time flies] like [an arrow]]

the system will gladly accept our new piece of information and respond with a fresh asterisk.

Extending Lolly: A Challenge

Even with the addition of some arithmetic capabilities, Lolly is quite limited. However, we can expand Lolly on our own and increase its capacity through the addition of new commands and knowledge structures.

To take a simple example, suppose we wanted to count references to a particular word or phrase in our knowledge base. We could use structures similar to DESCRIBE that would count the references instead of printing them out. For example, the procedure HOWMANY does this for us:

```
TO HOWMANY :item
PRINT (SENTENCE :item "appears COUNTPART :item :SENTENCE
    "times.)
PRINT []
END
```

```
TO COUNTPART :item :list
IF EMPTYP :LIST [OUTPUT 0]
IF MEMBERP :item THING FIRST :list [OUTPUT 1 + COUNTPART
    :item BF :list] [OUTPUT 0 + COUNTPART :item BF :list]
END
```

Using our personnel knowledge base we could enter

HOWMANY [I. Scott Tugo]

and the computer will print:

I. Scott Tugo appears 7 times.

Extensions of this sort are easy to create and, depending on your use for Lolly, you will probably make several of them. But a real challenge to your skills as a Logo programmer is to expand Lolly's power to let it make inferences. Because the material in the rest of this chapter is presented as a challenge, you may choose to read it as supplementary material, or you may accept the challenge to expand Lolly in the ways described. If you do accept the challenge, you will benefit from reading more about PROLOG first (see references in appendix 4). Even if you pass up the challenge, please read this section anyway; it may give you some insights into the tasks that face anyone who is creating a new computer language.

What is an inference? Right now Lolly knows only what it has been told—it can check for the occurrence of assertions. In our personnel knowledge base we have the assertion that Robin deCradle works for I. Scott Tugo and that I. Scott Tugo is the president of the company. From this information we can infer that Robin deCradle works for the president.

As it presently stands, Lolly can't make this conclusion because it lacks the ability to make the inference that X works for Z if X works for Y and Y is Z. In this form of an inference, we use the letters X, Y, and Z as pronouns because the relationship would hold for anyone who worked for I. Scott Tugo, or it would work for those people who worked for vice presidents, etc.

An inference can take many forms. For example, the inference

[X likes X]

just says that all people like themselves. For example, if we entered

DOES [John likes John]

the computer would respond with

Yes

if the inference was available in the system.

Sometimes an inference can be used to define a new relationship. For example,

```
[[X [is boss of] Y] IF
    [Y [works for] X]]
```

(List forms are used for the arguments in this inference as a hint we can use when creating our own implementation of an inference structure.) This inference makes the first assertion true ([X [is boss of] Y]) if it can verify the existence of the second assertion ([Y [works for] X]). For example, if we have an assertion that John works for Mary, then this piece of knowledge could be used to confirm that Mary is the boss of John.

We could also create an inference form for our original example:

```
[[X [works for] Z] IF
    [X [works for] Y] AND
    [Y is Z]]
```

In this case, the first assertion is true only if both assertions after the word IF are true. Because the word IF can be used to separate the unknown from the presumed, we might want to restrict our inferences to this form for simplicity in implementation.

How might one go about extending Lolly to let it make inferences? To start with, we need a command like ADD that allows relationships to be added to the knowledge base. We might call this new command INFER. Inferences might consist of two or more assertions in the form

[assert1 IF assert2]

or

[assert1 IF assert2 AND assert3 AND assert 4 . . .]

Each inference must have only one occurrence of IF. The assertions in each inference can contain "dummy variables" (or, as we have called them, pronouns) in the subject and object positions. We may want to restrict our pronouns to single capital letters such as U, V, W, X, Y, and Z. This gives us quite a few with which to build our inference structures. Just as ADD builds lists named S1, S2, S3, etc., we might want to store inferences as a set of lists labeled I1, I2, I3, etc. Once these structures have been built, we will need to modify our other Lolly commands.

For example, if we asked

DOES [John likes Philip]

the DOES command would first search the assertions to see if this assertion is present. If it is not present, then, instead of printing

No answer.

it will look at the list of inferences to see if any of them have the verb likes in an assertion appearing to the left of the word IF. For example:

[[X likes Y] IF [Y likes pizza]]

Then X and Y need to be temporarily replaced by John and Philip, and [Philip likes pizza] must be searched for in the list of assertions. If it is found, the computer would print YES; otherwise it would continue searching the list of inferences for other relationships using the verb likes. If none existed, or if they all failed to be verified, then No answer would be printed instead.

Compound inferences using the word AND would only be true if all the assertions to the right of the word IF are verified.

Keep in mind that assertions to the right of IF might be verified by still other inferences, so we must keep track of the rule we are testing while the system searches for other rules to apply. The use of names like S1, S2, S3, . . . and I1, I2, I3 . . . in separate lists facilitates this task because we can always keep track of where we are in a search.

Just as DOES needs to be modified, so do ASK and DESCRIBE. These are also nontrivial modifications, but they are good challenges to our skills as Logo programmers.

If you are interested in even more challenges, you might want to modify your system still further to implement a feature called "query the user." To take our example, suppose the system contained the inference that

[[X likes Y] IF [Y likes pizza]]

If we asked

DOES [Mary likes Sue]

a "query-the-user" system might ask *us* the question

Does Sue likes pizza?

If we enter Yes, then the system would automatically enter

[Sue likes pizza]

as an assertion and use this assertion to confirm that Mary likes Sue. One of the features of this system is that it lets information be gathered from the user as it is needed. In such a system we could start with a set of inferences and no assertions. As the system was used, assertions would be added to the knowledge base incrementally, and a carefully tailored system would result from these queries.

As systems grow large and complex, you may not immediately be able to see how a particular conclusion was drawn. To handle such cases, languages like PROLOG have a special primitive called **WHY**. (This is another tricky one to implement, but it can be done in Logo.) This command could be typed immediately after the system has drawn a conclusion and will provide a "trace" of the process by which the conclusion was drawn.

For example, if we entered

DOES [[I. Scott Tugo] is president]

the system would print **Yes.** If we entered

WHY

the system would print

Because you told me that [I. Scott Tugo] is president.

(indicating that the proof was by assertion). On the other hand, if the system were asked to confirm

DOES [Mary likes Sue]

the system might produce this result for **WHY:**

Because I have the inference [X likes Y] IF [Y likes pizza]
and Y is Sue
and X is Mary
and you told me that Sue likes pizza
therefore Mary likes Sue.

As I said before, don't worry about implementing these modifications to Lolly. The goal is to awaken you to the power of some new programming languages such as PROLOG and SOLO and to convince you that it is possible to create such powerful programming languages from Logo.

The next time someone tells you that Logo is just a graphics language for kids, let him or her read the previous two chapters of this book!

In our final chapter we explore Logo's interaction with the outside world—a topic deserving of special emphasis.

X. Logo and the Outside World

You might think it strange that I would wait for the last chapter to describe Logo's interaction with the outside world. After all, Logo conveys its results through the interaction between the screen and the user, and we as users communicate with Logo through our interaction with keyboards and other devices. Rather than being the last topic for consideration, such interactions might logically be thought to be the very first things we should explore.

In fact, there are some good reasons for waiting until now to explore this topic in depth. First, I have already introduced quite a few of the Logo primitives that let us display information on the screen and retrieve information from the keyboard. The main reason for waiting this long to cover this subject in depth is that I wanted you first to have a grasp of Logo's intrinsic computational power and a taste of the wide domain of applications for which it is suited. In this way you are better prepared to take advantage of the myriad ways Logo can interact with the outside world.

In computer parlance, we might think of any communication to or from the computer itself to be an interaction with a peripheral device. Viewed in this context, peripheral devices would include keyboards, displays, printers, plotters, disk drives, and graphics tablets. Some of these devices are designed for input only (keyboards and graphics tablets), some are for output only (displays, plotters, and printers), and some are for both input and output (disk drives). We will start with a review of the ways we communicate with Logo through the display and keyboard, and we will then explore the creation of a free-hand sketching system that uses a graphics tablet. The printing and plotting of text and graphic images are covered next, and I will conclude with a brief discussion of Logo's workspace and file management tools.

Working with the Screen and Keyboard

Logo's display screen can be configured in any of several ways. Text can be displayed in one of two modes: with either 40 or 80 characters across the screen (SETWIDTH 40 or SETWIDTH 80). Attempts to set the screen to another width (e.g., SETWIDTH 65) will result in an error message. Logo does not let us mix 40- and 80-column text on the same screen, and the screen will clear each time we issue the SETWIDTH command.

Three major display modes are available: TEXTSCREEN (abbreviated TS), which displays up to 24 lines of text; SPLITSCREEN (abbreviated SS), which displays four lines of text at the bottom of the screen and devotes the remainder to graphics; and FULLSCREEN (abbreviated FS), which devotes the entire display screen to graphics. A shorthand approach for getting to SPLITSCREEN is to hold the control key down and press the S key (CTRL S). The text screen can be obtained by pressing CTRL T.

What text characters are available to us? We already know that the screen will show the full complement of uppercase and lowercase letters, the numerals, and a wide assortment of punctuation marks. To see all the characters that are normally displayed on the screen, use the following procedure:

```
TO DISPCHARS :num
IF :num > 255 [STOP]
PRINT (SE [Character] :num [produces a] CHAR :num)
DISPCHARS :num + 1
END
```

The primitive CHAR is an operation that returns a character whose value is given by a number between 0 and 255. The reason for limiting the number of characters to 255 is that this limit corresponds to the information that can be stored in one byte of memory. Because bytes are the building blocks of the computer's memory (the Apple IIc and IIe have 128 thousand of them available for use), it is sensible to let each character occupy only one byte. The code that assigns characters to numbers is called the ASCII code, and it is fairly standard among computers.

To see the characters available for our computer we should enter

DISPCHARS 0

A succession of letters and numbers will begin to flash on the screen. This sequence will be repeated a few times, and for the last half of the numbers the characters will appear inverted—as dark characters on a light background. The first 32 characters are called control characters because they correspond to characters that would be typed when the control key is held down while typing. Although these characters are visible on the display, they generally will not be printed when sent to a printer. In fact, control characters are sometimes used to send special instructions to peripheral devices, so they should be used cautiously.

We wouldn't want to make a habit of it, but we could print all our messages using the **CHAR** operation. For example,

PRINT (WORD CHAR 72 CHAR 101 CHAR 108 CHAR 108
    CHAR 111)

will produce

Hello

on the screen. We obviously have better ways of typing text, but the **CHAR** operation is very handy when we want to send a control character to a peripheral.

Characters normally are printed next to previously printed characters or at the left edge of a new line. In fact, we can instruct Logo to place characters anywhere on the screen. To do this we must first reposition the cursor with the **SETCURSOR** command, which places the text cursor at a screen position whose coordinates are contained in a list. The first number in the list contains the column in which the cursor will be located (from 0 to 79), and the second number indicates which row will be used.

This command can be used to let us display text that is centered on the screen. For example, we could create a small piece of poetry that is stored as a list of lines:

```
MAKE "POEM [[The touch of Fall] [Will leave its mark] [In the
    varied color] [Of the dry leaves] [And we shall rejoice] [Not
    because the leaves are dying] [But because they free the trees
    to bloom again] [In the Spring]]
```

We can print this poem in the normal fashion with the following procedure:

```
TO POEMPRINT :list
IF EMPTYP :list [STOP]
PRINT FIRST :list
POEMPRINT BUTFIRST :list
END
```

If we were to enter

```
SETWIDTH 80
POEMPRINT :POEM
```

the following display would appear on our screen:

```
The touch of Fall
Will leave its mark
In the varied color
Of the dry leaves
And we shall rejoice
Not because the leaves are dying
But because they free the trees to bloom again
In the Spring
```

Now let's see what it takes to print this poem so it is centered on our 80-column screen. We must print each line so that the *x*-position of the cursor is offset to the left of center by half the number of characters in each line. The following procedure will do this for us:

```
TO CENTERPRINT :list
IF EMPTYP :list [STOP]
SETCURSOR LIST (40 − ((SIZE FIRST :list) / 2)) (LAST CURSOR)
PRINT FIRST :list
CENTERPRINT BUTFIRST :list
END

TO SIZE :list
IF EMPTYP :list [OUTPUT 0]
OUTPUT 1 + (COUNT FIRST :list) + SIZE BF :list
END
```

The only structural difference between **CENTERPRINT** and **POEMPRINT** is the addition of the **SETCURSOR** command. This command has the primary function of locating the *x*-coordinate of the cursor so that each line will be offset to the left of the center (column 40) by enough to center the line. The offset amount is half the number of characters that appear in each line of text. We use the procedure **SIZE** to count the number of characters. This procedure starts with a list of words and counts the letters in each word in the list, adding 1 to each word length to account for spaces between words. The recursive form of **SIZE** is reminiscent of the **LENGTH** procedure we used earlier in this book.

To see how well this set of procedures works, enter

```
CLEARTEXT
CENTERPRINT :POEM
```

This will produce the following centered listing on the screen:

The touch of Fall
Will leave its mark
In the varied color
Of the dry leaves
And we shall rejoice
Not because the leaves are dying
But because they free the trees to bloom again
In the Spring

Procedures like **CENTERPRINT** show the total control we can exercise in the display of information on the screen. We can test our skills by creating a procedure that aligns the poem against the right edge of the screen like this:

The touch of Fall
Will leave its mark
In the varied color
Of the dry leaves
And we shall rejoice
Not because the leaves are dying
But because they free the trees to bloom again
In the Spring

Thus far we have used two Logo primitives that let us communicate with the computer through the keyboard, **READ-LIST (RL)** and **READCHAR (RC)**. The major difference between these operations is that **READLIST** outputs a list of everything that was typed until the return key was pressed. For brief responses **READLIST** is quite adequate, but we can't use it for accepting more than 128 characters of information at a time. If we want to accept a list of typed information that is arbitrarily long, we can build a procedure that will do this job for us:

```
TO READLONG
OUTPUT PARSE GETIT READCHAR
END
```

```
TO GETIT :word
IF EQUALP :word CHAR 13 [PRINT :word OUTPUT '']
TYPE :word
OUTPUT WORD :word GETIT READCHAR
END
```

READLONG operates similarly to READLIST, except that it does not limit us to 128 characters in the list. The GETIT procedure recursively builds a word from characters typed at the keyboard until the return key (CHAR 13) was pressed. The resulting Logo word is then parsed into a list before being passed out of the READLONG operation. To test this procedure enter

```
PRINT READLONG
```

and enter the following text (without pressing return until reaching the end).

This is a test of a very long line of information. We can type several lines of text without pressing the RETURN key, and the system will accept it with no arbitrary limit of 128 characters being imposed by the system.

When we press return we will notice a pause as the list is assembled and printed. READLONG does behave differently from READLIST in several ways. First, there is the noticeable time delay for long entries. For very long entries it is possible to temporarily run out of memory, in which case Logo will present us with an error message. Also, some of the keys behave differently from the way they behave in READLIST. For example, if we press the delete key while we are typing we will see a special character on the screen instead of the deletion of the preceding character. As a challenge, we can modify GETIT to check for such keystrokes and to respond correctly. As a hint, we will need to know the ASCII code for the delete key. The code for any character can be found by using the Logo primitive ASCII as shown in the following procedure:

```
TO KEYTEST
PRINT ASCII READCHAR
KEYTEST
END
```

Of Turtles and Koalas

Although the keyboard may remain our primary input device for Logo, there are numerous other tools we can use to convey information to the computer. The KoalaPad touch tablet connects to the joystick port and allows the computer to sense the position of a finger or stylus on the table surface.

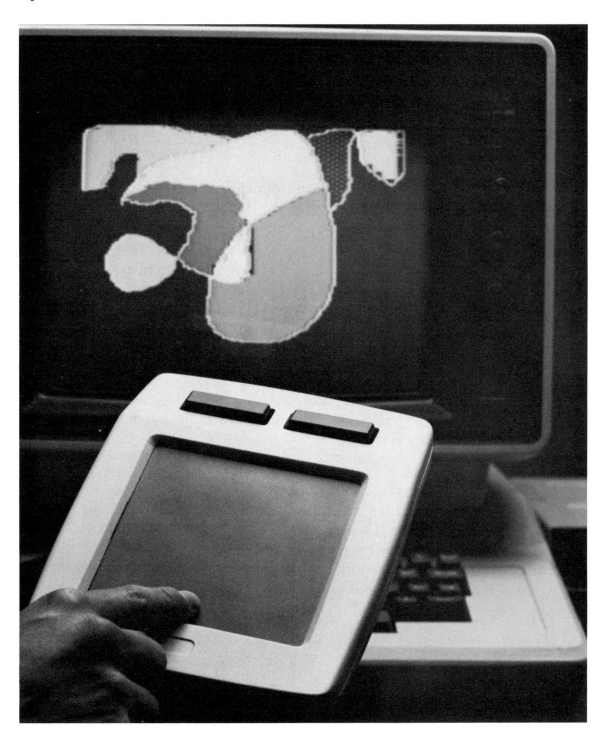

The tablet contains a 4¼-inch square surface for measuring finger or stylus position and two buttons that can be sensed as well. The *x*-coordinate of the KoalaPad is sensed with the Logo primitive PADDLE 0, and the *y*-axis is sensed with PADDLE 1. To see how the KoalaPad operates, connect the tablet to the computer's joystick port and run the following procedure:

```
TO TABLET
PRINT SE (PADDLE 0) (PADDLE 1)
TABTEST
END
```

When this procedure is executed, two columns of numbers will appear on the screen. The first number corresponds to the value of the *x*-coordinate and the second corresponds to the value of the *y*-coordinate. If we are not touching the tablet surface, the numbers we see correspond to the tablet's "release state." These numbers will typically be in the vicinity of 7. As we run a finger or stylus over the tablet surface we will see these numbers change up to a maximum value in the mid-200s. The *x*-values increase from left to right, and the *y*-values increase from top to bottom.

In addition to reading stylus position on the tablet, Logo lets us read the state of the two tablet buttons. The primitive BUTTONP returns TRUE when a button is pressed. The state of the left button is sensed with BUTTONP 0, and the right button is sensed with BUTTONP 1.

The program's ability to sense finger position on a surface lets us construct many interesting programs. Perhaps the most obvious application is the creation of a sketching program that lets us create free-hand drawings on the display screen. The simplest sort of drawing program will move the turtle on the display screen in response to the tablet coordinates, will place the pen down if a button is pressed, and will pick it up otherwise.

To correctly map the tablet coordinates to those on the screen, we can use the two procedures TABX and TABY:

```
TO TABX
OUTPUT 1.1 * ((PADDLE 0) — 128)
END

TO TABY
OUTPUT 128 — (PADDLE 1)
END
```

TABX scales the *x*-coordinate data to insure that the turtle will have the entire range of the screen on which to move. TABY changes the tablet data so that the top of the tablet surface corresponds to the top of the display screen. To draw lines on the screen, we can use the following simple procedure:

```
TO SDRAW
IF BUTTONP 0 [PENDOWN] [PENUP]
SETPOS SENTENCE TABX TABY
END
```

To test this procedure enter

```
.SETSCRUNCH 1
CS FULLSCREEN SDRAW
```

This will clear the screen and display a flashing turtle image. As we move a finger or stylus on the screen we will see the turtle follow this motion on the screen. To draw a line, move the turtle to a starting point and then hold down the left button while drawing. Release the button when the line is finished.

The following sketch was made using this procedure.

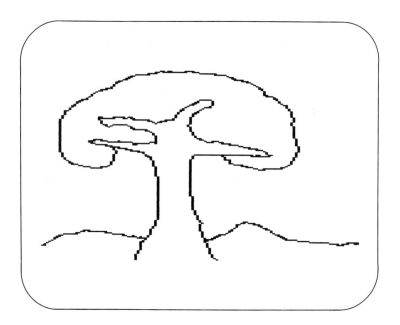

Although this sketching program demonstrates the ability of Logo to use alternate input devices such as the KoalaPad, we can create a more powerful illustration system that might be of more use.

A complete illustration system ought to let us draw pictures in color and let us have access to powerful features such as area fill and color changing. It should also let us clear the screen and save and load pictures from memory.

To minimize our use of the keyboard, the illustration system we will devise makes use of a menu at the bottom of the graphics screen. This menu contains several square boxes to indicate paint pots for various colors as well as boxes for the erasure, saving, and loading of pictures.

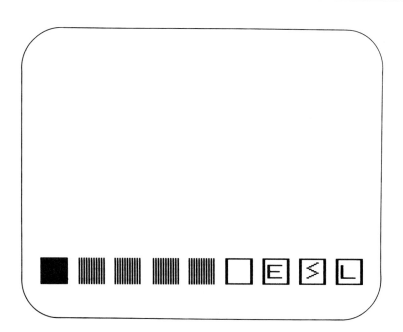

With the menu at the bottom of the screen, the bulk of the screen is free for the creation of our picture.

The main procedure for our system will be called **PAINT**. Its job is to initialize the program, draw the paintpots and the option boxes, and start the main drawing procedure:

```
TO PAINT
PAINTPOTS
OPTIONS
DRAW
END
```

The first two procedures used by **PAINT** are shown here:

```
TO PAINTPOTS
HT PU SETPC 1 FS WINDOW .SETSCRUNCH 1 SETPOS
     [−130 −90]
SETPAINTS 1
SETPC 1
END
```

```
TO SETPAINTS :num
IF EQUALP :num 6 [STOP]
PD SETPC :num SQUARE 20 RT 45 FD 5 FILL BK 5 LT 45 PU
RT 90 FD 30 LT 90
SETPAINT :num + 1
END

TO SQUARE :size
REPEAT 4 [FD :size RT 90]
END

TO OPTIONS
PD SQUARE 20 PU
RT 90 FD 30 LT 90
PD SQUARE 20 PU E
RT 90 FD 30 LT 90
PD SQUARE 20 PU S
RT 90 FD 30 LT 90
PD SQUARE 20 PU L
ST
END

TO E
FD 5 RT 90 FD 5 PD
FD 10 BK 10 LT 90 FD 10
RT 90 FD 10 BK 10 LT 90
BK 5 RT 90 FD 7 BK 7 LT 90
PU BK 10 LT 90 FD 5 RT 90
END

TO S
PU FD 5 RT 90 FD 7 PD
LT 30 FD 8 LT 120 FD 8 RT 120 FD 8
PU RT 180 FD 8 LT 120 FD 8 RT 120 FD 8 RT 30 FD 7 RT 90 BK 5
END

TO L
FD 5 RT 90 FD 5 PD
FD 10 BK 10 LT 90 FD 10
PU BK 15 LT 90 FD 5 RT 90
END
```

PAINTPOTS clears the screen, sets the aspect ratio, and uses SETPAINTS to draw the colored squares at the bottom of the screen to show where the color menu is located. OPTIONS draws four black boxes and places the letters E (for erase), S (for save picture), and L (for load picture) in each of the last three boxes. The procedures E, S, and L simply draw the letters in a somewhat crude but recognizable form.

The DRAW procedure is a simple variant of our original drawing procedure, SDRAW:

```
TO DRAW
IF BUTTONP 0 [PENDOWN] [PENUP]
IF BUTTONP 1 [IF (LAST POS) < −75 [CHPAINT] [PD FILL PU]]
SETPOS SENTENCE TABX TABY
DRAW
END
```

The procedure uses the left button to indicate whether the pen is to be raised or lowered. The right button serves two functions. If the cursor is in the picture area, pressing this button will fill an area with the currently chosen color. If the cursor is in the menu area, control is passed to the CHPAINT procedure, which checks to see which box contains the cursor and either changes the color to the value associated with the selected box or performs one of the special functions (erase, save, or load):

```
TO CHPAINT
IF (FIRST POS) < −110 [SETPC 1 BOUNCE STOP]
IF (FIRST POS) < −80 [SETPC 2 BOUNCE STOP]
IF (FIRST POS) < −50 [SETPC 3 BOUNCE STOP]
IF (FIRST POS) < −20 [SETPC 4 BOUNCE STOP]
IF (FIRST POS) < 10 [SETPC 5 BOUNCE STOP]
IF (FIRST POS) < 40 [SETPC 0 BOUNCE STOP]
IF (FIRST POS) < 70 [CS PAINTPOTS OPTIONS BOUNCE STOP]
IF (FIRST POS) < 100 [SAVESCREEN STOP]
IF (FIRST POS) < 130 [LOADSCREEN STOP]
END
```

CHPAINT uses a set of IF commands to look up the proper response from a table. The BOUNCE procedure "debounces" the button press by waiting for the button to be released before returning to the next command:

```
TO BOUNCE
IF OR BUTTONP 0 BUTTONP 1 [BOUNCE]
END
```

The procedures that save and load the screens from the disk use the Logo primitives LOADPIC and SAVEPIC as shown below:

```
TO SAVESCREEN
SPLITSCREEN
LOCAL :name
CT HT
PR [Enter name of picture to be saved.]
MAKE "name FIRST READLIST
MAKE "name WORD :name ".pic
PR SE "Saving :name
SAVEPIC :name
ST FULLSCREEN
END

TO LOADSCREEN
SPLITSCREEN
LOCAL :name
CT
PR [Enter name of picture to be loaded.]
MAKE "name FIRST READLIST
MAKE "name WORD :name ".pic
PR SE "Loading :name
LOADPIC :name
FULLSCREEN
END
```

This set of procedures now gives us a complete illustration system to experiment with. Remember that the FILL command fills an area bounded by the fill color.

To use the system, just enter

PAINT

and sketch away!

The following picture was created with this system.

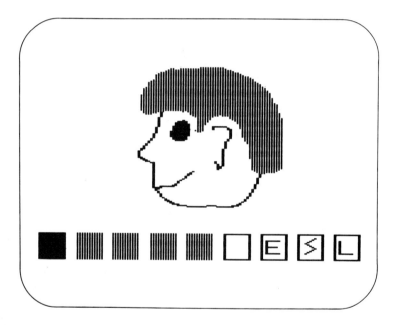

From this starting point we can further tailor the PAINT system to fit special needs. For example, we can add some more menu items to let us draw straight lines, circles, etc.

Farewell Sweet Prints

In addition to directing Logo's output to the display screen, we can send it to the Image Writer printer. To use this printer with the Apple IIe requires the Apple Super Serial Card. No extra card is required for the Apple IIc.

Logo output can be directed to the printer as either text or a picture. Text is directed to the printer through the Logo DRIBBLE command, which takes an argument that corresponds to the slot containing the serial interface card. For the IIe computer this card is most often located in slot 1. In this case, we can print Logo output by giving the command

DRIBBLE 1

before issuing any PRINT commands. After this command is entered, anything that we type or that Logo prints on the screen will also be sent to the printer. The only exception to this is if we enter the procedure editor. To turn off the DRIBBLE function we must enter the command

NODRIBBLE

Suppose we wanted to print a list of the files that are on a diskette. To get a listing on the printer we would only need to type:

DRIBBLE 1 CATALOG NODRIBBLE

As soon as return is pressed, the disk catalog will appear on both the display screen and the printer. To get a listing of all the procedures and global variables in the workspace, enter

DRIBBLE 1 POALL NODRIBBLE

If we want to see titles instead of listings, we can enter POTS instead of POALL. For variable names we can enter PONS, and for procedure listings only, we can enter POPS.

This use of the printer justifies its connection to Logo. But in fact the Image Writer can be used for much more than book-keeping functions. It can also be used to print the output of text-generating programs.

The printer will always print the text that appears on the screen, but it will not always print it in the screen's format. For example, the procedure CENTERPRINT will center the text on the screen but will not print text in centered form with the printer. Similarly, special commands can be sent to the printer to influence the size of printed letters, and these changes will not be reflected in the size of the characters that appear on the display screen. For example, we can select headline (double-width) type by entering

DRIBBLE 1 PRINT CHAR 14

before printing something on the printer. To return to normal-sized type, we can enter

PRINT CHAR 15

Numerous other printer features are available to us through the use of a series of "escape sequences," which are pairs of characters sent to the printer for the purpose of setting a particular mode. The first character in the sequence is ESC, which is entered by printing CHAR 27. To take advantage of these various printer modes from Logo, we will want to define the following operation:

TO ESC
OUTPUT CHAR 27
END

The Image Writer manual shows how to use escape se-quences to do everything from picking new character sets to underlining text, setting horizontal and vertical tabs, reversing the direction of line feeds, and even controlling the direction of print-head motion. To select an escape sequence, we must have the printer selected (with the DRIBBLE command) and then enter a line like:

PRINT WORD ESC CHAR 88

(This command will cause all future text to be underlined as it is printed.) To turn off the underlining, enter

PRINT WORD ESC CHAR 89

A valuable printer procedure that resets the printer to its starting settings is shown here:

```
TO RESTORE.PRINTER
DRIBBLE 1
PRINT WORD ESC CHAR 99
NODRIBBLE
END
```

Now that we know how to print text in interesting ways, we should know how to get a copy of our turtle graphic images printed. This is accomplished with the command PRINTPIC. If the serial card is in slot 1 (for a IIe computer), or the printer is plugged into jack 1 on the IIc, we would print your screen images by entering

PRINTPIC 1

PRINTPIC prints your picture exactly as it appears with FULLSCREEN, even if we have drawn it with the SPLIT-

SCREEN option. This means that no text will appear on the picture.

We should keep in mind two useful tips as we use PRINTPIC. First, much finer lines will appear in the printout if we first set the background "color" to 6 before drawing a picture and if we use only pen color 1:

```
SETBG 6
SETPC 1
```

Second, we will find that the correct aspect ratio for the printer is probably different from that for the display screen. To print squares that look like squares instead of rectangles, we should invoke the following command before drawing any picture that is to be printed.

```
.SETSCRUNCH 1.0
```

Because we will most likely want to print only one image per page, we might want to use a procedure that prints the picture and then gives a form-feed command (CHAR 12) to eject the page:

```
TO SCREEN
PRINTPIC 1
DRIBBLE 1 PRINT CHAR 12 NODRIBBLE
END
```

All the screen images shown in this book were created with this procedure.

The Plot Thickens   There is no question that the Image Writer printer is a valuable tool for capturing Logo artwork; however, there are two major limitations to this device. First, because it prints images using the same resolution as the display screen, diagonal lines are replete with "jaggies" that can interfere with the quality of the printed image. Second, the Image Writer can print pictures in only one color. Fortunately, another option is available, and that is to create pictures using the Apple Color Plotter. This peripheral connects to the Apple serial port in a similar fashion to the Image Writer, and it is available with a disk of utilities that lets it be used with Logo. The plotter has four pens (black, red, green, and blue) that are controlled with the **SETPC** command.

The plotter is used quite differently from the Image Writer printer. When the Image Writer is used, the picture is created on the screen first, and then the printer is instructed to make a copy on paper. The plotter starts with a blank screen, and the picture is drawn on the plotter at the same time as it is drawn on the display screen.

To use the plotter, we must first load the file called **STARTUP** from the plotter disk. This file contains all the routines needed to send turtle-graphic commands to the plotter as well as to the screen. We must include the command **PLOT** before giving any commands to the turtle, or nothing will be plotted on the plotter. When a picture is finished, the plotter can be "disconnected" from Logo by issuing the command **NO-PLOT**.

The printer and plotter can be compared side by side with the following procedures:

```
TO TREE :size :angle
IF :size < 1 [STOP]
LEFT :angle
FORWARD :size TREE :size * 0.61803 :angle BACK :size
RIGHT 2 * :angle
FORWARD :size TREE :size * 0.61803 :angle BACK :size
LEFT :angle
END
```

```
TO TREEDEMO
.SETSCRUNCH 1
SETBG 6 HT CS
REPEAT 2 [TREE 45 45 RT 180]
SCREEN
END

TO TREEPLOT
PLOT
HT CS
REPEAT 2 [TREE 45 45 RT 180]
NOPLOT
END
```

The procedure **TREEDEMO** creates a pattern on the screen and prints it on the Image Writer printer, and **TREEPLOT** creates the same picture on the color plotter. The next two figures show the results of these procedures.

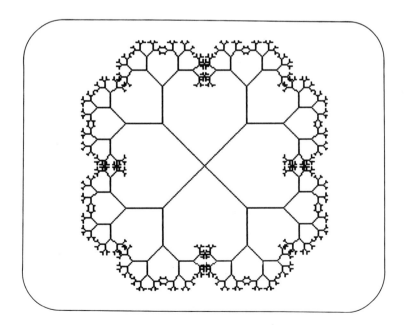

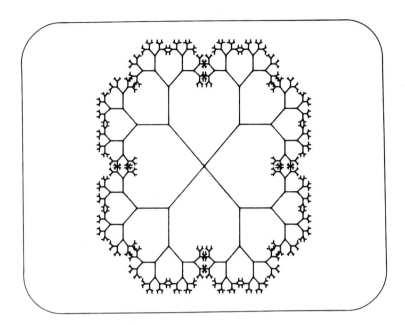

The major difference between the two drawings is the virtual absence of "jaggies" in the picture created with the plotter. The difference in aspect ratio between the two pictures is an artifact of the version of the plotter software I was using at the time the picture was created.

Logo Workspaces and Files

The Logo workspace consists of that portion of a computer's random-access memory devoted to the storage of procedures and global variables. Changes in this workspace are made anytime a procedure or a variable name is made or erased. The size of available workspace is measured in *nodes*. Many other computer languages, such as BASIC, measure free memory in *bytes*. A byte contains eight binary digits (bits) and is the amount of storage needed to contain one ASCII character. In this version of Logo, a node is five bytes long. The rationale behind memory storage in nodes is beyond the scope of this book, but it can be found in technical articles on the implementation of languages like LISP and Logo.

To see how many nodes are available in our workspace, we can give the command:

PRINT NODES

This number may seem quite small at times, and yet we may be able to run a lengthy program. The reason for this is that when Logo uses a node, it makes note of which nodes are no longer needed as procedures finish their tasks. If the node space becomes severely cramped, Logo then executes a "garbage collection," which frees these unused nodes to be used again. The garbage-collection process can be detected as a slight (and occasionally annoying) pause in the execution of procedures. If we want to force a garbage collection ourselves (to insure that a time-critical procedure runs without interruption, for example), we can enter the command

RECYCLE

just before starting the procedure.

When procedures are saved on a disk, the contents of Logo workspace are transferred into a *program file* on the diskette. Program files are one of four types of disk files that are supported by Apple Logo II. The others are *picture files, dribble files,* and *data files*. All these files are referenced through a ProDOS path name. The details of path-name manipulation and creation are explained in careful detail in the Logo manual, so they will not be discussed (or used) here.

The principal tools for working with program files are the commands SAVE, LOAD, and ERASEFILE. The present contents of workspace can be saved by giving a command such as:

SAVE "FRACTALS

This command will save everything in the present Logo workspace under the file name FRACTALS. Before saving the file, Logo first checks to make sure the name FRACTALS hasn't already been used. (This keeps the user from accidentally erasing a file.) To erase an old version of a file before saving the new one (a risky proposition if you live in an area with frequent power outages), we should enter

ERASEFILE "FRACTALS SAVE "FRACTALS

Both commands can be typed on the same line so we don't have to wait for one task to finish before starting the next. The safest way to save an updated copy of workspace is to save it once under a dummy name, erase the old file, and save it again under the old file name. In this way at least one revision of the procedures will always be available.

Program files are loaded from the disk through the **LOAD** command:

LOAD "FRACTALS

When **LOAD** is executed, it does not erase the contents of the workspace first, which means that any procedures and variables in the loaded file will be added to those already present in the workspace. What happens if we already have a procedure or variable whose name is the same as that of one being loaded from the disk? In this case, the old version of the procedure or variable is replaced by the new one! The fact that **LOAD** lets us append new procedures into our workspace is quite handy. Suppose there is a collection of useful procedures that we want to make part of every workspace we use. These procedures can be saved in a special file and loaded into our workspace anytime without erasing our present procedures.

Sometimes we may want to save only the values of our variables on the disk and erase all the procedures. One way to do this is to give the command

ERPS

(ERase ProcedureS) before saving the workspace. Procedures can be stored without any variable values by using **ERNS** (ERase NameS) instead. Most disk space, however, is taken up with a wide variety of procedure files.

The files that take a lot of disk space are the picture files, which consist of the raw bit patterns that generate the graphic images on the display. To remind us that these files contain pictures and not procedures, we might want to append the suffix .PIC to the file name when they are created. To save a picture file (as we did with the KoalaPad program), we would give the command:

SAVEPIC "MYDRAWING.PIC

Pictures saved with **SAVEPIC** take much more disk space than pictures saved as the Logo procedures that generated them. But **SAVEPIC** pictures are often recreated on the screen much faster than they were created by the original turtle-graphic procedures. Picture files can be loaded into the system with the command **LOADPIC**. When a picture is brought into the computer's display, any previous image on that display is replaced by the new one. This means that if we want to add a turtle-graphic image to a previous image saved with **SAVEPIC**, we must load the picture file first and then run the new turtle-graphics procedures. As with other disk files, unused picture files can be erased with **ERASEFILE**.

We have already encountered dribble files when we illustrated the use of the Image Writer printer. Instead of directing keyboard entries and Logo procedure results to a printer, **DRIBBLE** can be used to save this information on a diskette. For example, the command

DRIBBLE "TYPESCRIPT

will place anything the user or the system prints on a disk file named TYPESCRIPT. This collection process will continue until a **NODRIBBLE** command is received. Only one dribble file may be open at a time, so a device must be chosen carefully. For example, if we want to capture a Logo session on disk and print it out later, we can dump the contents of a dribble file to the printer with the procedure:

```
TO DUMPIT :filename
DRIBBLE 1
POFILE :filename
NODRIBBLE
END
```

The command **POFILE** prints out the contents of a file to the screen. If we want to copy one file to another, we can create a procedure to do this for us:

```
TO COPYFILE :destination :source
DRIBBLE :destination
POFILE :source
NODRIBBLE
END
```

This is a more powerful version of **DUMPIT**, because it lets us dump information to a printer as well as to another disk file.

The properties of data files are sufficiently well covered in the Logo manual to eliminate the need for their elaboration here. The ability of Apple Logo II to handle disk files gives it considerable utility, and you will want to take advantage of this capability as you make further explorations on your own.

Back at the beginning of this book I made the claim that there was much more to Logo than just turtle graphics. I hope that as you read this book you not only reached the point where you agreed with me but that you also became familiar enough with Logo that you could see how valuable a tool it can be for your own programs. I also hope you discovered how much fun Logo can be as a tool to help you think about the process of thought itself.

Thank you for letting me share my enthusiasm for this language with you.

Appendix 1:
Apple Logo II Startup and Operation

Setting Up Logo II

The mechanical details of starting Logo II are covered quite adequately in the various manuals that accompany the language, so they won't be repeated here. Instead I will concentrate on some tips and stylistic details as they pertain to this book and to Logo in general.

It is important to create one or two blank formatted disks on which to store your Logo procedures. If there is a formatted disk available to us before we start programming we can avoid the frustration of having created some terrific programs and then finding out that we have nowhere to save them.

The **FORMAT** file on the Logo master diskette contains a disk-formatting utility we can use with Logo, and it is already installed in the computer. Alternatively, we can format disks directly from ProDOS using the ProDOS utilities diskette. When formatting a blank disk we are asked to supply a volume name. If this name is different from **LOGO**, we must use the **SETPREFIX** command to set Logo to the new disk name before we save or retrieve files with it. Although it is safer for each disk to have its own volume name, the use of **SETPREFIX** every time we want to change a disk can be tiresome. If we are using only one disk drive and are careful to remove the Logo master diskette as soon as Logo has loaded, we will save ourselves a lot of time by giving our disks the name LOGO when they are formatted.

A formatted ProDOS diskette holds a lot of information. In fact, all the procedures in this book fit easily on one diskette. Because diskettes are inexpensive, we should always save important program files on two diskettes and print out a listing of all our procedures as well. This way, if a disk gets ruined by a power failure during a **SAVE** command or some other catastrophe strikes, our programs will be intact. I know all too well the penalty for ignoring this suggestion!

When Apple Logo II is started on the Apple IIe, the text screen is set for 40-column lines. With the Apple IIc we can set the startup mode to 40- or 80-column lines with the 40/80 switch on the top of the computer case. The setting of characters per line can be changed anytime we want through the **SETWIDTH** command.

You may already have noticed that Apple Logo II is case insensitive. This means we can enter **FORWARD**, **forward**, **Forward**, **FoRwArD**, or any other combination of uppercase and lowercase letters and Logo will understand that we want it to execute the command **FORWARD**. Logo variables are case insensitive as well. For example, if we enter

MAKE "VALUE 6

and then enter

PRINT :value

6 will appear on the screen. In fact, the only times Logo makes a distinction in its interpretation of uppercase and lowercase letters is when we are referring to a ProDOS directory and when we are referring to a literal word. For example,

SETPREFIX "/LOGO

is not the same as

SETPREFIX "/logo

and

EQUALP "HOUSE "house

is FALSE.

Even though case doesn't matter for procedures and variable names, Logo will keep track of entries in the same way we entered them.

This gives us an opportunity to use a handy convention in our procedure listings. In this book all procedures and global variables have been defined using uppercase letters, and the names of local variables have been defined using lowercase letters. Although this convention has no special meaning for Logo, it does lend a certain flair and readability to our listings.

Another listing convention that has been adopted in this book (but not in Logo itself) is the indentation of continued long lines. When entering a long line into Logo, it is important that the return key not be pressed until the end of the line is reached, no matter how many characters of text may appear on the screen. For lines that would run past the edge of the page, our indentation of long lines shows that the return key should not be pressed until the end of the last indented line. For example, in the following procedure the return key should be pressed at the end of MESSAGE, at the end of the list (lines.]), and after the word END:

```
TO MESSAGE
PRINT [This example of a very long message illustrates our
    convention regarding the indentation of long lines.]
END
```

Although we can create procedures in Logo by typing TO procedurename, etc., long procedures and procedures with lots of similar lines are much easier to create with Logo's editor. The Logo manuals illustrate the use of this editor in depth, and users should become familiar with it before creating long Logo procedures.

Appendix 2:
Digressions on Sundry Topics

Variables Revisited   As mentioned in chapter 2, the concept of a variable can be a bit tricky. A key to understanding this concept is to understand the difference between the name of something and the thing named. For example, we can build a model of the Logo **MAKE** command using file folders. Anytime we want to create a variable by issuing a command such as

MAKE "MEMBERS 6

we can think of this process as though Logo is creating a file folder whose name on the tab is **MEMBERS** and that contains a sheet of paper with the number 6 on it.

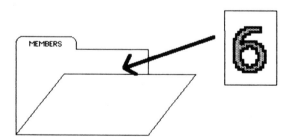

Every time we create a new variable it can be thought of as the creation of a new folder, each of which has its own contents.

The name appearing on the tab of a folder can be referred to by its literal name—a word preceded by a quotation mark. The contents of a folder can be read by using the Logo primitive **THING** or by replacing the quotation mark with a colon (:).

So when we enter

PRINT THING "MEMBERS

or

PRINT :MEMBERS

this instructs Logo to find the folder whose name is
MEMBERS, open it, and print its contents on the screen.
For our example, the contents of MEMBERS is the number 6.

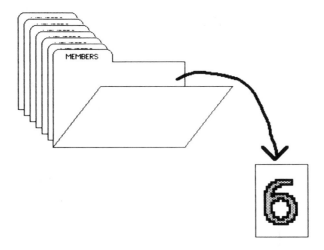

The contents of a folder can be anything—a number, a
word, a list of words, another variable name, a list of procedure names. In fact, the file folder metaphor is an accurate representation of how we use file folders in the real world.
Information pertaining to a certain topic is gathered together
and stored in a folder. Each folder has a name, and its contents
can be examined, altered, and even destroyed. If we have a
folder named NEWSPAPER CLIPPINGS, we know that its

name is NEWSPAPER CLIPPINGS, and that its content is likely to be articles that have been cut from newspapers. We have no trouble distinguishing between the name of the folder and its contents. Variables work the same way.

However, the distinction between the name of something and the thing named is not always obvious, as shown in this ancient Sufi tale told by Idries Shah:

After a long journey, Nasrudin found himself amid the milling throng in Baghdad. This was the biggest place he had ever seen, and the people pouring through the streets confused him.

"I wonder how people manage to keep track of themselves, who they are, in a place like this," he mused.

Then he thought, "I must remember myself well, otherwise I might lose myself."

He rushed to a caravanserai. A wag was sitting on his bed, next to the one which Nasrudin was allotted. Nasrudin thought he would have a siesta, but he had a problem: how to find himself again when he woke up.

He confided in his neighbor.

"Simple," said the joker. "Here is an inflated bladder. Tie it around your leg and go to sleep. When you wake up, look for the man with the balloon, and that will be you."

"Excellent idea," said Nasrudin.

A couple of hours later, the Mulla awoke. He looked for the bladder, and found it tied to the leg of the wag. "Yes, that is me," he thought. Then, in a frenzy of fear he started pummeling the other man: "Wake up! Something has happened, as I thought it would! Your idea was no good!"

The man woke up and asked him what the trouble was. Nasrudin pointed to the bladder. "I can tell by the balloon that *you* are *me*. But if *you* are *me*—who, for the love of goodness, AM I?"

(From *The Exploits of the Incomparable Mulla Nasrudin* by Idries Shah, Designist Communications, 1983.)

Looping vs. Recursion

At first glance, tail-end recursion may behave in a manner that makes it hard to distinguish from looping, which is the simple repetition of a series of commands. For example, in languages like BASIC looping is accomplished through use of the GOTO command or a better form known as the FOR . . . NEXT loop. In Logo the looping construction is REPEAT; it is a good idea to know when a procedure should use tail-end recursion or make use of the REPEAT command. The general rule is that REPEAT should be used when a set of commands are to be repeated with fixed values for all variables and the commands are to be repeated a fixed number of times. Otherwise, a recursive form of the procedure is preferred.

For example, we can draw a square with either of the following two procedures:

```
TO SQUARE :size
REPEAT 4 [FD :size RT 90]
END
```

```
TO SQUARE :size
FD :size RT 90
SQUARE :size
END
```

From the standpoint of what appears on the screen, both procedures produce the same result except that the recursive procedure will continue forever. In this case the preferred construction involves looping with the REPEAT command.

But if it is our intention to create a square spiral, the recursive form of the procedures is preferred. For example, the following two procedures can be used to create the same figure:

```
TO SQRSPI :size
IF :size > 100 [STOP]
FD :size RT 90
SQRSPI :size + 1
END
```

```
TO SQRSPI :size
MAKE "INDEX :size
REPEAT 100 [FD :INDEX RT 90 MAKE "INDEX :INDEX + 1]
END
```

Both versions will produce the same figure if we enter:

SQRSPI 1

The second form is more cumbersome than the first, because
the value of the dummy variable **INDEX** must be recalculated
each time the instructions are repeated. Contrast this with the
recursive form (shown first) in which each successive use of the
procedure is simply passed a different value for the variable
:size.

The results of a procedure that uses tail-end recursion can
be accomplished through looping, but this is not the case for
procedures that use embedded recursion.

More Fractals

An unlimited number of fractal curves can be modeled in Logo.
The book by Mandelbrot listed in appendix 4 shows numerous
examples for your computational pleasure. In this section we
will further explore the simple Koch curve fractal that we
created in chapter 3.

The curve we explored was made from a triangular bump
with straight lines on either side:

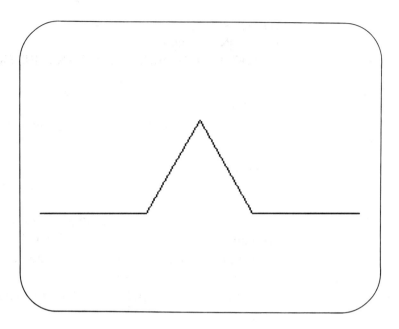

What would we get if this triangle were replaced by a square bump, or by a pentagonal one? We can explore these questions be creating a procedure that lets us make any fractal whose "bump" is constructed from a regular polygon. To design this procedure we need to examine some general properties of the starting curve. First, the bump will be made from all but one side of the polygon that defines its shape. If the polygon has N sides, then the bump will have $N - 1$ sides. Second, the turtle must be turned to the left before it draws the bump. The amount by which it must be turned can be calculated from the fact that the net turning angle for the curve is zero. The two left turns (one at each end of the bump) must balance out all the right turns used in making the bump. Each of the bump turns will have a value of $360 / N$, and there will be $N - 2$ of them. Because the left turns must be divided equally between both left turns, the amount of each left turn will be $360 * (N - 2) / (N * 2)$.

From this information we can construct a procedure that will create any polygonal Koch curve we wish:

```
TO KOCH :num :size :limit
IF :size < :limit [FD :size STOP]
KOCH :num :size / 3 :limit
LT 360 * (:num - 2) / (:num * 2)
REPEAT (:num - 1) [KOCH :num :size / 3 :limit RT (360 / :num)]
LT 360 / :num
LT 360 * (:num - 2) / (:num * 2)
KOCH :num :size / 3 :limit
END
```

(The second left-turn command is used to remove an extra right turn created inside the REPEAT command.)

To see the operation of this procedure, we need to be able to set the cursor to our desired location for starting the picture. This is accomplished with the following procedure:

```
TO SETUP :poslist
CS
PU SETPOS :poslist PD RT 90
END
```

Because we already know the result for a triangular bump, let's explore the curves that result when the bump is square:

```
SETUP [-121 -60] KOCH 4 243 243
SETUP [-121 -60] KOCH 4 243 81
SETUP [-121 -60] KOCH 4 243 27
SETUP [-121 -60] KOCH 4 243 9
SETUP [-121 -60] KOCH 4 243 3
```

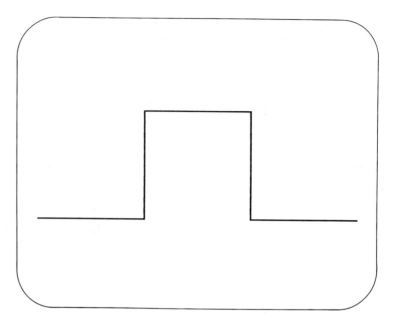

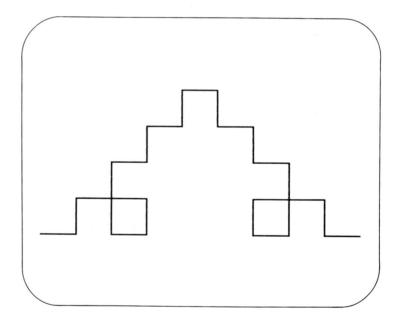

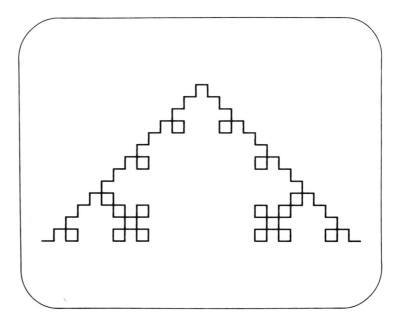

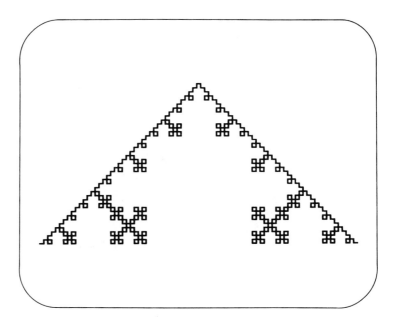

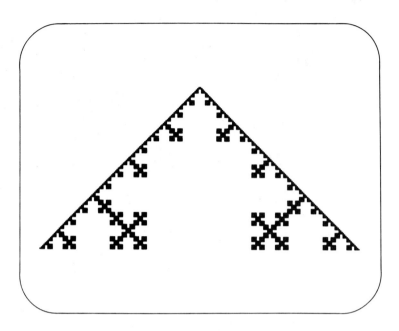

The figures produced for a square bump are quite attractive, and their shapes are not immediately obvious from inspection of the generating curve. To further explore the properties of these curves, the following figures show the starting and developed forms for bumps with larger numbers of sides. These figures were generated with the following commands:

```
SETUP [−121 −60] KOCH 5 243 243
SETUP [−121 −60] KOCH 5 243 9
SETUP [−81 −70] KOCH 6 162 162
SETUP [−81 −70] KOCH 6 162 6
SETUP [−81 −70] KOCH 7 162 162
SETUP [−81 −70] KOCH 7 162 6
```

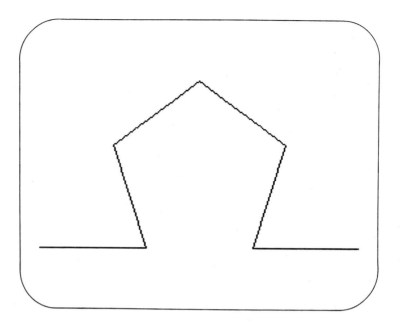

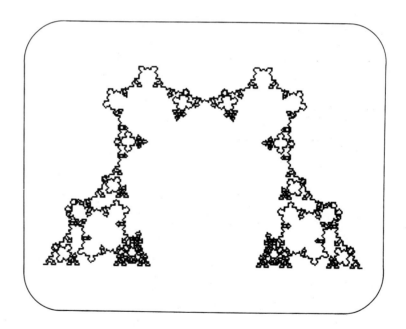

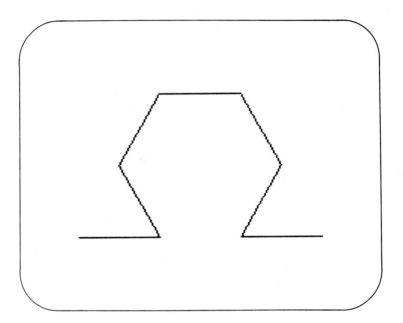

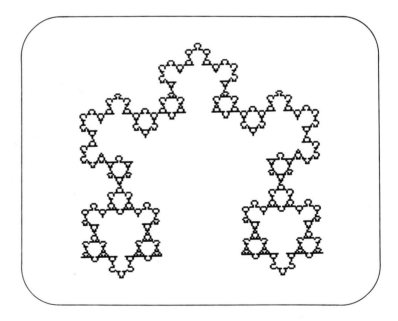

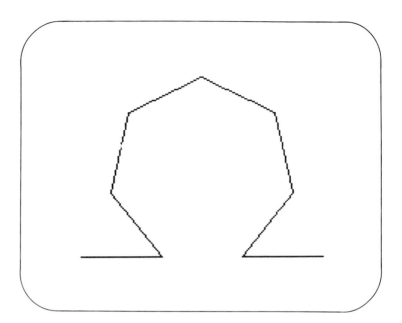

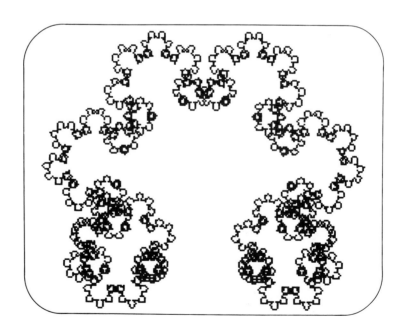

Appendix 3: Description of the Logo Primitives Used in This Book

This appendix contains an alphabetical list of the Logo primitives used in this book. Each primitive is listed in dictionary form and belongs to one of three parts of Logo's "speech": commands (*cmd*), operations (*oper*), and predicates (*pred*). These can be used to build user-defined procedures (**proc**) that are treated by Logo as if they were primitive words in the language. The arguments used by these primitives include numbers (:number), words (:word), lists (:list), and general objects such as words, lists, and numbers (:object). The definition associated with each primitive is intentionally brief. The chapter in which each primitive is defined or first used is included at the end of each definition.

AND :pred1 :pred2   *pred*: Returns TRUE only if both :pred1 and :pred2 are TRUE (ch. 6).

ARCTAN :number   *oper*: Returns the angle in degrees whose tangent is given by :number (ch. 4).

ASCII :word   *oper*: Returns the ASCII code of the character stored in :word (ch. 10).

BACK :number   *cmd*: Moves the turtle backward :number units. Abbreviated BK (ch. 3).

BEFOREP :word1 :word 2   *pred*: Returns TRUE if :word1 is before :word2 alphabetically (ch. 5).

BUTFIRST :object   *oper*: Returns all but the first element in :object. Abbreviated BF (ch. 5).

BUTLAST :object   *oper*: Returns all but the last element in :object. Abbreviated BL (ch. 5).

BUTTONP :number   *pred*: Returns TRUE if paddle button in position :number is pressed down (ch. 10).

CATALOG   *cmd*: Prints catalog of current disk path name on the screen (ch. 10).

CHAR :number   *cmd*: Returns character whose ASCII code is :number (ch. 10).

CLEAN   *cmd*: Erases the graphics screen without relocating the turtle (ch. 3).

CLEARSCREEN   *cmd*: Clears the graphics screen and relocates the turtle to the home position. Abbreviated CS (ch. 2).

COS :number   *oper*: Returns the cosine of :number degrees (ch. 4).

COUNT :object   *oper*: Returns the number of elements in :object (ch. 5).

CURSOR   *oper*: Returns a list of coordinates for the text cursor (ch. 5).

DEFINE :word :list   *cmd*: Defines Logo procedure named :word containing instructions present in :list (ch. 6).

DIFFERENCE :number1 :number2   *oper*: Returns the difference of :number1 and :number2. Infix form is - (ch. 4).

DOT :list   *cmd*: Places a dot on the graphics screen at the coordinates contained in :list (ch. 3).

DOTP :list   *pred*: Returns TRUE if screen contains a dot at coordinates in :list (ch. 3).

DRIBBLE :number   *cmd*: Directs the output of Logo commands and procedures to the file given by :number (ch. 10).

EDNS   *cmd*: Lets all global variable values and names be edited (ch. 10).

EMPTYP :object   *pred*: Returns TRUE if :object is empty (ch. 5).

ERALL   *cmd*: Empties the Logo workspace of all procedures and variables (ch. 10).

ERASE :word   *cmd*: Erases procedure named :word from the workspace. Abbreviated ER (ch. 10).

ERASEFILE :word   *cmd*: Erases file stored in :word from the disk (ch. 10).

ERN :object   *cmd*: Erases any variables whose names are in :object (ch. 8).

ERPS   *cmd*: Erases all procedures from the workspace (ch. 10).

EQUALP :object1 :object2   *pred*: Returns TRUE if :object1 and :object2 are equal. Infix form is = (ch. 5).

FILL *cmd*: Fills an enclosed area with the current pen color (ch. 6).

FIRST :object *oper*: Returns first element in :object (ch. 5).

FORWARD :number *cmd*: Moves the turtle forward :number units. Abbreviated FD (ch. 3).

FPUT :object :list *oper*: Returns list containing :list in front of which :object has been inserted (ch. 5).

FULLSCREEN *cmd*: Allows graphics to be displayed on entire screen (ch. 10).

HEADING *oper*: Returns the turtle's heading in degrees (ch. 3).

HIDETURTLE *cmd*: Removes the turtle's image from the screen. Abbreviated HT (ch. 3).

HOME *cmd*: Moves the turtle to its home position and orientation without clearing the screen (ch. 3).

IF pred :list1 (:list2) *cmd*: Executes the commands in :list1 if pred is TRUE, and otherwise executes commands in optional :list2 (ch. 3).

INT :number *oper*: Returns the integer part of :number (ch. 4).

INTQUOTIENT :number1 :number2 *oper*: Returns the integer part of the quotient of :number1 and :number2 (ch. 4).

ITEM :number :object *oper*: Returns the *n*th element in :object where *n* is given by :number (ch. 5).

LAST :object *oper*: Returns the last element in :object (ch. 5).

LEFT :number *cmd*: Turns the turtle to the left by :number degrees. Abbreviated LT (ch. 3).

LIST :object1 :object2 *oper*: Returns a list containing :object1 and :object2, preserving their internal forms (ch. 5).

LISTP :object *pred*: Returns TRUE if :object is a list (ch. 5).

LOAD :word *cmd*: Loads program file stored in :word from the disk (ch. 10).

LOADPIC :word *cmd*: Loads binary picture file named :word (ch. 10).

LOCAL :object *cmd*: Makes variable names stored in :object local to the procedure in which this command appears (ch. 4).

LOWERCASE :word *oper*: Returns :word with all lowercase letters (ch. 6).

LPUT :object :list *oper*: Returns list containing :list to which :object has been appended (ch. 5).

MAKE :word :object   *cmd*: Assigns :object as to the contents of a variable named :word (ch. 2).

MEMBER :object1 :object2   *oper*: Returns portion of :object2 that starts with :object1 (ch. 6).

NODES   *oper*: Returns number of free nodes in the Logo workspace (ch. 10).

NODRIBBLE   *cmd*: Terminates redirection of Logo output to any device set up with the **DRIBBLE** command (ch. 10).

NOT pred   *pred*: Returns **FALSE** if pred is **TRUE** and **TRUE** if pred is **FALSE** (ch. 6).

NUMBERP :object   *pred*: Returns **TRUE** if :object is a number (ch. 5).

OR :pred1 :pred2   *pred*: Returns **TRUE** if either :pred1 or :pred2 is **TRUE** (ch. 6).

OUTPUT :object   *cmd*: Passes :object out of a procedure. Abbreviated **OP** (ch. 4).

PADDLE :number   *oper*: Returns value corresponding to the position of a game paddle or similar device in location :number (ch. 10).

PARSE :word   *oper*: Returns list containing :word (ch. 5).

PEN   *oper*: Returns the state of the pen—**PU**, **PD**, etc. (ch. 3).

PENCOLOR   *oper*: Returns current pen color (ch. 3).

PENDOWN   *cmd*: Lowers the turtle's pen. Abbreviated **PD** (ch. 3).

PENUP   *cmd*: Lifts the turtle's pen. Abbreviated **PU** (ch. 3).

POALL   *cmd*: Prints out the entire contents of the workspace (ch. 10).

POFILE :word   *cmd*: Prints out the contents of the file whose name is stored in :word (ch. 10).

PONS   *cmd*: Prints out names and values of all global variables in the workspace (ch. 10).

POPS   *cmd*: Prints out all procedures in the workspace (ch. 10).

POS   *oper*: Returns a list of x- and y-coordinates of the turtle (ch. 3).

POTS   *cmd*: Prints out titles of all procedures in the workspace (ch. 10).

PRINT :object   *cmd*: Prints the contents of :object on the screen (ch. 2).

PRINTPIC :number   *cmd*: Prints the contents of the graphics screen on a graphics printer located in port :number (ch. 10).

PRODUCT :number1 :number2   *oper*: Returns the product of :number1 and :number2. Infix form is * (ch. 4).

QUOTIENT :number1 :number2   *oper*: Returns the quotient of :number1 and :number2. Infix form is / (ch. 4).

RANDOM :number   *oper*: Returns a random integer between 0 and :number − 1 (ch. 4).

READCHAR   *oper*: Waits for key to be pressed and then returns a word containing the character that was pressed. Abbreviated RC (ch. 8).

READLIST   *oper*: Returns a list containing anything entered at the keyboard and terminated with a RETURN. Abbreviated RL (ch. 5).

RECYCLE   *cmd*: Performs garbage collection of unused nodes (ch. 10).

REMAINDER :number1 :number2   *oper*: Returns the remainder after the integer division of :number1 by :number 2 (ch. 4).

REPEAT :number :list   *cmd*: Repeats the commands in :list by :number times (ch. 3).

RERANDOM   *cmd*: Resets random number generator (ch. 4).

RIGHT :number   *cmd*: Turns the turtle to the right by :number degrees. Abbreviated RT (ch. 3).

ROUND :number   *oper*: Returns the integer closest to :number (ch. 4).

RUN :list   *cmd*: Executes Logo commands in :list (ch. 6).

SAVE :word   *cmd*: Saves contents of the workspace on disk under the filename :word (ch. 10).

SAVEPIC :word   *cmd*: Saves the binary image of the graphics screen on disk under the filename :word (ch. 10).

SENTENCE :object1 :object2   *oper*: Returns a list combined from :object1 and :object2 (ch. 5).

SETCURSOR :list   *cmd*: Sets the text cursor to coordinates stored in :list (ch. 10).

SETPC :number   *cmd*: Sets the pen color to :number (ch. 3).

SETPOS :list   *cmd*: Sets the turtle to the coordinates stored in :list (ch. 3).

SETPREFIX :word   *cmd*: Sets Logo to communicate with the file directory stored in :word (ch. 10).

SETSCRUNCH :number   *cmd*: Sets the aspect ratio of the graphics display to :number (ch. 3).

SETWIDTH :number   *cmd*: Sets the text display to either 40 or 80 columns, depending on the value of :number (ch. 6).

SETX :number   *cmd*: Sets the *x*-coordinate of the turtle to :number (ch. 3).

SETY :number   *cmd*: Sets the *y*-coordinate of the turtle to :number (ch. 3).

SHOWNP   *pred*: Returns TRUE if the turtle is showing (ch. 3).

SHOW :object   *cmd*: Prints :object on the screen and leaves outer brackets in place if :object is a list (ch. 5).

SHOWTURTLE   *cmd*: Makes the turtle image visible on the screen (ch. 3).

SIN :number   *oper*: Returns the sine of :number degrees (ch. 4).

SPLITSCREEN   *cmd*: Splits the display screen into an upper graphics portion and a lower text portion (ch. 10).

SQRT :number   *oper*: Returns the square root of positive :number (ch. 4).

STEP :object   *cmd*: Starts the stepwise execution mode for procedures whose names are in :object (ch. 3).

STOP   *cmd*: Stops execution of a procedure and returns to calling procedure or top level (ch. 3).

SUM :number1 :number2   *oper*: Returns the sum of :number1 and :number2. Infix form is + (ch. 4).

TEXT :word   *oper*: Returns the list of instructions that define the procedure named :word (ch. 6).

TEXTSCREEN   *cmd*: Sets display for full display of text only (ch. 8).

THING :word   *oper*: Returns the contents of the variable named :word (ch. 2).

THROW :word   *cmd*: Diverts execution of the procedure to the label named :word (ch. 6).

TOOT :number1 :number2   *cmd*: Produces a tone with frequency given by :number1 and duration given by :number2 (ch. 7).

TOWARDS :list   *cmd*: Turns turtle to face towards coordinates contained in :list (ch. 7).

TRACE :object   *cmd*: Starts trace function for procedure names in :object (ch. 3).

TYPE :object   *cmd*: Prints :object on screen without moving to a new line when done (ch. 6).

UNSTEP :object   *cmd*: Stops the stepwise execution mode for procedures named in :object (ch. 3).

UNTRACE :object   *cmd*: Stops trace function for procedures named in :object (ch. 3).

UPPERCASE :word   *oper*: Returns :word with all uppercase letters (ch. 6).

WAIT :number   *cmd*: Suspends execution of the next Logo command for :number jiffies where 1 jiffy is 1/60 second (ch. 6).

WINDOW   *cmd*: Allows the turtle to move off the display screen (ch. 7).

WORD :word1 :word2   *oper*: Returns the word combined from :word1 and :word2 (ch. 5).

WORDP :object   *pred*: Returns TRUE if :object is a word (ch. 5).

WRAP   *cmd*: Restricts the turtle's movements to the display screen and causes the turtle to reappear at the opposite edge of the screen if it is moved off (ch. 7).

XCOR   *oper*: Returns the *x*-coordinate of the turtle (ch. 3).

YCOR   *oper*: Returns the *y*-coordinate of the turtle (ch. 3).

Appendix 4: Books I Wish I Could Have Read Before Learning Logo (and Some I Wish I Had Time to Read Now)

Philosophy of Programming and Problem Solving

Allen, J., R. Davis, and J. Johnson. *Thinking about [TLC] Logo: A Graphic Look at Programming with Ideas.* Holt, Rinehart and Winston, 1984.

Brooks, F., Jr. *The Mythical Man Month: Essays on Software Engineering.* Addison-Wesley, 1975.

Papert, S. *Mindstorms: Children, Computers, and Powerful Ideas.* Basic Books, 1980.

Polya, G. *How to Solve It: A New Aspect of Mathematical Method.* Princeton University Press, 1973.

Smith, H., and T. Green, eds. *Human Interaction with Computers.* Academic Press, 1980.

Thornburg, D. *Exploring Logo Without a Computer.* Addison-Wesley, 1984.

Turtle Geometry

Abelson, H., and A. diSessa. *Turtle Geometry: The Computer as a Medium for Exploring Mathematics.* MIT Press, 1981.

Thornburg, D. *Discovering Apple Logo: An Invitation to the Art and Pattern of Nature.* Addison-Wesley, 1983.

Recursion

Hofstadter, D., *Gödel, Escher, Bach: An Eternal Golden Braid.* Basic Books, 1979.

Kim, S. *Inversions.* Byte Books/McGraw Hill, 1981.

Mandelbrot, B. *The Fractal Geometry of Nature.* W. H. Freeman, 1982.

Artificial Intelligence

Boden, M. *Artificial Intelligence and Natural Man.* Basic Books, 1977.

Bundy, A., ed. *Artificial Intelligence: An Introductory Course.* North-Holland, 1978.

DeKoven, B. *The Well Played Game: A Player's Philosophy.* Anchor/Doubleday, 1978.

Dreyfus, H. *What Computers Can't Do: The Limits of Artificial Intelligence.* Harper/Colophon, 1979.

Feigenbaum, A., and P. McCorduck. *The Fifth Generation: Artificial Intelligence and Japan's Computer Challenge to the World.* Addison-Wesley, 1983.

Hofstadter, D., and D. Dennett. *The Mind's I, Fantasies and Reflections on Self & Soul.* Basic Books, 1981.

Sagan, C. *The Dragons of Eden: Speculations on the Evolution of Human Intelligence.* Random House, 1977.

Shah, I. *The Exploits of the Incomparable Mulla Nasrudin.* The Octagon Press, Ltd., 1983.

Turkle, S. *The Second Self: Computers and the Human Spirit.* Simon and Schuster, 1984.

Walter, W. Grey. *The Living Brain.* W. W. Norton, 1953.

Watzlawick, P. *How Real is Real? Communication, Disinformation, Confusion.* Random House, 1976.

Weizenbaum, J. *Computer Power and Human Reasoning, From Judgement to Calculation.* W. H. Freeman, 1976.

Winston, P. *Artificial Intelligence.* Addison-Wesley, 1977.

Other Languages Worth Knowing

Clark, K., and F. McCabe. *Micro-PROLOG: Programming in Logic.* Prentice-Hall, 1984.

Clocksin, W., and C. Mellish. *Programming in Prolog.* Springer-Verlag, 1981.

Ennals, R. *Beginning Micro-PROLOG.* Harper & Row, 1984.

Goldberg, A., and D. Robson. *Smalltalk-80: The Language and Its Implementation.* Addison-Wesley, 1983.

Touretzky, D. *LISP: A Gentle Introduction to Symbolic Computation.* Harper & Row, 1984.

Winston, P., and B. Horn. *LISP.* Addison-Wesley, 1981.

Yazdani, M. *New Horizons in Educational Computing.* Halsted Press, 1984.

Index